HOW TO IMPROVE YOUR PREACHING

HOW TO IMPROVE YOUR PREACHING

By

BOB JONES, Jr.

Litt.D., L.H.D., LL.D.

NEW YORK

Fleming H. Revell Company

LONDON AND EDINBURGH

New York: 158 Fifth Avenue
London: 16 Anerley Hill

FOREWORD

PEOPLE WHO WRITE BOOKS on etiquette have my sympathy.
They must—poor creatures—find little pleasure at a dinner
party. I have often wondered if, when dining out with
friends, they are not on such a strain to observe all the rules
of etiquette which they have laid down that they are unable
either to concentrate upon the conversation or enjoy a good
meal. When one presumes to set down rules of practice in
any art—and etiquette is certainly a fine art—he immediately becomes the object of observation when he, himself,
attempts to practice it, and must perforce be at great pains
to follow his own rules and set an example of what he has
prescribed for others.

It is with this in mind that I have sought wherever possible in this volume to avoid setting down certain rules
which a preacher should follow in the conducting of a service
or the preaching of a sermon. I have thought it best to discuss certain general principles and to suggest some helpful
technical aids in developing an effective and forceful pulpit
style. Where it has seemed necessary to set forth a rule
either in the construction of sermons or in pulpit speech
and manner, I have done so with a mental reservation to
violate such rules in my own preaching whenever I feel the
violation will make a sermon more effective. While it is
generally wise to observe them, there are occasional circumstances which make it more advisable to set them aside.

The suggestions offered and the few rules laid down will,
I believe, prove valuable, particularly to the young preacher
and to the man who, though he has been for some time in
the ministry, has never had the opportunity of a seminary

education. Every effort has been made to present the material concisely and simply and to avoid technical terms wherever possible. When it has been necessary to use such terms they are clearly defined.

Only gifts divinely given, carefully trained, and deeply consecrated, combined with an earnest study of God's Word and a great and burning zeal and passion, will make a man a *great* preacher. But it is not a man's responsibility to be a great preacher. It is his duty to be the best preacher *he* can be. To that end he should seek to develop his natural gifts, however limited, and pray earnestly for a full measure of that zeal without which knowledge is dead and for that love without which even the most eloquent of speakers becomes as "sounding brass and tinkling cymbals."

B. J., Jr.

Cleveland, Tennessee.

CONTENTS

CONTENTS

I

"PREACH THE WORD"

"Go ye into all the world, and preach the Gospel to every creature," was our Lord's commission to His disciples. Preaching was to be their first duty and most important work. The preaching of the Gospel is still the obligation of His church, and preaching should certainly be the main business of a minister of the Gospel. The sermon should be the very center of the service. It is through the foolishness of preaching that it pleases God to save them that believe.

Great and decisive preaching has characterized every period of growth and revival and power the church of Christ has experienced. Periods of declension and coldness and defeat have been periods of poor and uninspired preaching. The great reformers, who in the power of the Holy Spirit, warmed cold hearts, quickened dead ecclesiasticism, and set the church upon a path of conquest for her Lord, were men of great power in the preaching of the Word.

Nothing is more indicative of the apostacy of our own day than the scarcity of powerful preaching. Not only is the general level of preaching poor, but *great* preaching is almost extinct. Possibly this condition is due to the fact that ours is a day of slight conviction. No man can be a great preacher who is not dominated by great convictions —conviction that men are lost in sin and Christ is able to save them, conviction that he himself is called of God to give to dying men the Word of life. Revival fires are never kindled under the preaching of men who are not completely convinced of the inspiration of God's Word, deeply con-

9

cerned for the salvation of souls, and fully conscious of their responsibility to give men the Gospel.

Some congregations that go to church Sunday after Sunday never hear a sermon, for much that is called preaching is not that at all. A book review is not a sermon, though it be spoken from a pulpit. Discussion of current events does not become a sermon by echoing in vaulted Gothic arches. A discourse on social ills cannot by some strange mutation be transformed into a sermon simply because it is uttered by a doctor of divinity. A sermon is the proclamation of the Word of God. Any discourse which is not based upon God's Word is not a sermon according to the accepted definition of the term, for Webster defines a sermon as: "A discourse delivered in public, usually by a clergyman, for the purpose of religious instruction, and grounded on a passage of Scripture." Speaking from a pulpit is not preaching in the Scriptural sense unless it involves a proclamation of the Truth of God.

Some years ago a minister, apparently desiring publicity, suggested in the public press that a moratorium be declared on preaching for a year or two in order that preachers might have a better opportunity to evaluate their own beliefs and improve the quality of their messages, and that the congregations might, in the interim, form some opinions for themselves and listen with rested minds when preaching should be resumed. It is impossible to imagine such a suggestion coming from an individual called of God to the proclamation of the Gospel and fired by a passion for the lost. Actually, however, in some churches such a moratorium on preaching has existed for many years. Their pulpits have not been silent, however, but have echoed to the vain words of man's wisdom instead of to the declaration and interpretation of the sure Word of God. They have sounded forth lovely treatises on nature and art. Expressions of ethics and philosophy have been offered to the hungry-hearted congregations, stones to those who need bread, but there has been no *preaching* from those pulpits in years. It is no wonder that in so many churches attendance has fallen off tremendously.

There are some men of forceful personality, keen of mind and fluent of speech, who Sunday after Sunday will attract great throngs by reason of their own great gifts. Such men are now—as they have always been—in the minority. The average preacher cannot expect great throngs to come Sunday after Sunday to hear *him* unless he has a message from God's Word which is addressed to the needs of their hearts and lives. In the discussion of current events and the analysis of world conditions he is neither so well informed nor so gifted a speaker as the radio commentator. Is it surprising then that people stay away from his service in great numbers? He is very foolish to attempt to compete on unequal ground with the trained experts whom the people can hear on the radio on such subjects.

The man who preaches with conviction the words of divine authority backed by a consistent life will always find a hearing. When our Lord was on earth the common people heard Him gladly because He "taught them as One having authority." A preacher of the Word of God has all the authority of heaven behind him. In a world where philosophies are in a state of flux, where human institutions are founded on the quicksands of human frailty, men need the divine certainty of "Thus saith the Lord." There can be no authoritative message except the message of God's Word. Organized Protestant Christianity as represented by the various great denominations has been largely losing its grip upon the minds and hearts of men because so many of its pulpits have failed to speak with the authority based upon the truth of Scripture. Higher criticism, "modernism," and so-called liberalism have denied the inspiration of the Word of God and sought to undermine its authority. Ministers, in an effort to be "cultured," and "modern," and "broad," have accepted unproved scientific theories instead of the Word, which is forever settled in heaven. They have expounded the guesses of men rather than the oracles of

God. Others have tried to ride the fence—to reconcile the one to the other. It cannot be done.

Miles Coverdale, who first printed the whole Bible in English, set down words of advice which might well be heeded by many of the learned divines of our own day, "If thou be a preacher and hath oversight of the flock of God, awake and feed Christ's sheep with a good heart, and spare no labor to do them good, . . . and be ever reading, exhorting, and teaching in God's Word, that the people of God run not to other doctrines, and lest thou thyself, when thou shouldest teach others, be found ignorant."

As preachers have neglected more and more the one source to which they can look for an authoritative message, the pulpit has been relegated to a place of less importance in our churches. Oftentimes this is true literally as well as figuratively, for in many churches of "evangelical" denominations which have departed from the faith or grown cold in heart the pulpit, following the tradition of liturgical ecclesiasticism, has been put to one side of the building and an altar placed in the center. Rituals have been substituted for reality. There has developed a form of godliness with a denial of its power. Without a positive proclamation of the Gospel to attract—without the food of the Word for hungry hearts—it has been felt necessary to build up an elaboration of ceremony, an overemphasis on pageantry, and color, and music. Pulpit discourse has become a small part of the service when it should occupy the chief place.

The preacher must address himself to the individual. There is no such thing as a "social Gospel." The Gospel is personal. Christ died to save sinners. This is the good news, but the sinners must be reached individually, and society cannot be reached except through the individual. Acceptance of the Gospel message and faith in the Lord Jesus Christ change the individual, set him apart from society as a whole. The Church is in the world, but not of the world. Society can never be redeemed en masse. Society can be

12

changed to some extent as the individuals who make up society have a change of heart through faith in Christ.

The Church is nowhere in the Bible commissioned to spend herself in the reformation of the world, and she is not commanded of her Lord to be primarily concerned with social evils. It is certainly not her main obligation to seek to solve the problems of society such as slum conditions, labor relations, or political corruption. The Church is the custodian of a Gospel which regenerates the individual.

In his epistle to Philemon, Paul discusses the relationship of the individual Christian master to his Christian slave, but Paul nowhere attacks the institution of slavery. The tendency in the present generation has been to attempt to apply the teachings of the Lord Jesus Christ to the lives of unregenerate men and women. It cannot be done. An unconverted world lacks the power to live up to the ethics which Christ sets forth. An unregenerate heart is not pure and cannot be expected to see God. It is the duty of the preacher to present to each individual his personal responsibility to God. Phillips Brooks once said, "Preaching is the communion of truth through a man to men." There can be no preaching of power which is not personal in application, which does not seek to change individual lives. Susanna Wesley, mother of great sons, wrote, "The true end of preaching is to mend men's lives and not to fill their heads with unprofitable speculation."

John Wycliffe, the morning star of the Reformation, defined preaching as something that should be "apt, apparent, full of true feeling, fearless in rebuking sins, and so address to the heart as to enlighten the spirit and subdue the will." Martin Luther in discussing preaching has the following to say:

"When he preaches on any article a man must first distinguish it, then define, describe, and show what it is; thirdly, he must produce sentences from the Scripture to prove and to strengthen it; fourthly, he must explain it by examples; fifthly, he must adorn it with similitudes; and lastly, he must admonish and arouse the indolent, correct the disobedient, and reprove the authors of false doctrine."

The man who proclaims God's Word must be fearless and regard no man. "For all have sinned, and come short of the glory of God," and each must be brought to repentance. Peter Cartwright, powerful preacher and yielded man of God, was preaching in a large church in the city of Nashville. In the midst of his discourse, as he was vigorously denouncing sin, he was interrupted by the pastor, who pulled his coat tail and whispered, "General Jackson has come in; General Jackson has come in!" Turning to the preacher, Cartwright replied in the same resonant tone in which he had been preaching. "Who is General Jackson? If he don't get his soul converted, God will damn his soul as quick as He will a Guinea Negro." * Rude and crudely put as this may have been, it represents the sort of fearlessness so often lacking in our pulpits.

Matthew Simpson said of the preacher:

" 'His throne is the pulpit;' he stands in Christ's stead; his message is the Word of God; around him are immortal souls; the Saviour, unseen, is beside him; the Holy Spirit broods over the congregation; angels gaze upon the scene, and heaven and hell await the issue. What associations, and what vast responsibility!" **

The great preachers have all been conscious of their responsibility to God and to their hearers. As a young man Whitefield heard a remark by a minister, which he never forgot, "I wish, whenever I go into the pulpit to look upon it as the last time I may ever preach, or the last time the people may hear me." Ever after Whitefield felt his responsibility as a preacher.

* Philip M. Watters, *Peter Cartwright* (New York: Eaton & Mains, 1910), p. 87.
** Matthew Simpson, *Lectures on Preaching,* (New York: Phillips & Hunt, 1879), p. 166.

14

The preacher truly called of God is a member of a glorious company. The heavenly Father has thought him worthy to put him in trust with the Gospel. Upon his proclamation of the Word of God hangs the destiny of souls, upon his interpretation of the Word may depend the decisions of men's hearts. Preaching the Gospel is the biggest business in the world. This is the day of opportunity. Men and women are hungry for the Gospel. Hearts are wide open for the reception of the Truth of God as revealed in His Word.

In one of the art galleries of Europe a young man stood enrapt before a portrait done by one of the great masters. As he looked his eyes filled with tears. Another visitor to the gallery noticed him standing there and said, "Young man, what troubles you?" Still gazing on the painting, the youth replied, "I can't paint like that. I never will be able to paint like that." Then his face brightened. "But, thank God," he said, "I am a painter too."

As we study the great sermons of the pulpit giants of the past and read of the skill and power of the mighty preachers whom God has so abundantly used, we may well feel like that young man. We may never be able to preach as they preached, but thank God we are called to the preaching of the same Gospel and the exaltation of the same Christ. We are preachers too!

II

TYPES OF SERMONS

IT IS POSSIBLE to classify sermons in a number of different ways. In his book *The Theory of Preaching,* Austin Phelps offers seven possible methods of classification, and the authors of all the standard works on homiletics have their own method. For all practical purposes, however, two general methods of classification seem sufficient—the first classification according to *style* and the second classification according to *purpose*. Under the first division we shall classify sermons according to their method of textual treatment and style of construction. Under the second classification we shall deal with the types of sermons according to the purpose which they are intended to accomplish when preached.

ACCORDING TO STYLE

Thought sermons. As we stressed in the previous chapter, all sermons should be founded upon the Word of God; that is, they should be based on Scripture, a verse, a portion of a verse, or a number of verses. The Scripture upon which the sermon is based is not, however, always treated in the same fashion. In the *thought sermon* the verse or phrase from a verse provides the theme or thought of the message. The idea of the sermon is found in the passage of Scripture. The sermon is the development of this idea or thought. For example, simple statements from the Bible, such as these, afford excellent texts for the thought type of sermon: "Where there is no vision the people perish," "God is love," "But Namaan was a leper," "In the beginning God." The sermon developed from such a text would not seek to expound fully or explain the text. It would, instead, simply take the statement as a thought around which the discourse should be built and would treat the text as suggesting the theme upon which the author's message would be established. Direct questions from the Bible afford excellent text for *thought sermons.* For example: "What will ye do with Jesus which is called Christ?" "To whom shall we go?" "Whom say ye that I am?" "What will ye do in the end?" are all thought-provoking texts. For a young preacher a message of this type is often one of the easiest to construct and preach. There is a general outline which can be used in the development of almost any such question: (1) the circumstances of the question, (2) answers which might be given to the question, (3) the correct answer to the question. However, such a simple and obvious outline is by no means always the best outline. The great difficulty in developing this type of message is, in fact, finding a fresh and original method of approach.

The *thought sermon* has been a great favorite with evangelists. J. Wilbur Chapman was particularly skillful in building sermons of this sort. Two of his greatest messages were *thought sermons* of a biographical nature: "And Peter," "And Judas Iscariot." These messages are excellent examples of this type of sermon. They are based upon a few words, an incomplete statement, a portion of a verse. It is well to remember, however, that as a general rule the use of such fragmentary Scripture portions is very dangerous, particularly for the preacher who is not a thorough student of Scripture, as one is liable to do violence to the meaning of the Bible, or use the Scriptural phrase simply as a springboard from which to leap into an expression of one's own thoughts and opinions without supporting quotations from the Bible to lend divine sanction and authority to the sermon. This very obviously is not good pulpit procedure. However, Mr. Chapman, as the reading of these two sermons will show, preached great and stirring sermons from these texts. The one deals with God's unfailing love and forgiveness. The other stresses the sin of the rejection of God's grace. Preaching a *thought sermon,* one will do well to remember the old adage: "A text without its context becomes a pretext," and it is wise in preaching such a sermon to set forth something of the context, the circumstances, and occasion on which the statement of the text was made, or the general theme of the paragraph from which the text is taken, and to give the listeners to understand the preacher does not intend to expound the text, but that he simply wishes to direct the attention of the congregation to the words of the text which shall be used as the basic thought for his message.

The subjects available for discussion in sermons of this

type are numberless and include both the concrete and material, and the abstract and the spiritual, but there should always be a personal and practical application of the subject to the lives and hearts of the hearers. While some authorities on homiletics object to spiritualizing a text, there seems to be no sound reason for refraining altogether from such a practice, when it often produces effective results, provided the practical application is made.

Suppose as an example of the *thought sermon* we take the subject "gifts," suggested by the text, "And opening their treasure, they offered unto him gifts." The preacher in his treatment of the text might deal with the kinds of gifts offered, the use to which such objects were generally put, why such gifts were appropriate for Christ (here he would deal with the implied and prophetic symbolism of the offering), and bring the subject directly home to his hearers by a discussion of the gifts which *they* owe to Him.

Expository sermons. The expository sermon expounds a portion of God's Word. That is to say, it opens up the meaning of that portion of Scripture and sets forth the truths therein taught. Expository preaching is generally considered the best type. Some ministers go so far as to suggest it is the only type which is really Scriptural and, therefore, fully effective. It is impossible to agree with such an extreme position. Expository preaching has a very positive and definite value and an important place in pulpit discourse. Certainly no minister should neglect it, but all ministers are not equally gifted in the art of exposition. Some who are richly talented and greatly used in the preaching of the *thought sermon* are incapable of good expository preaching. To say then that such men should refrain from developing and practicing their own style of sermon construction and their own effective preaching methods is to take an unreasonable position. To hold that expository preaching is the only type of preaching worthy of the name is to reflect upon Sunday, Chapman, Phillips Brooks, and many other great preachers.

In order to be a great expository preacher, a man must be gifted not only with a spiritual apprehension and insight into the meaning of Scripture but he must also be a gifted teacher. Inaccurate and unsound exposition obviously does more harm than good and is extremely dangerous. Dull exposition may be almost as bad, since those who are untaught in the Scripture, sitting under such a ministry may form the opinion that the Word of God is dull and uninteresting and its study laborsome and uninspiring. Every preacher should, however, cultivate whatever gift he may have along the line of Bible teaching, and so diligently study God's Word that he is familiar enough with it to give to it a sane and correct interpretation.

An expository sermon may treat a book, a chapter, a paragraph, a verse, or even a portion of a verse. Sometimes the whole passage will be read and no single verse taken as a text. In other cases a single verse or a portion of a verse may be taken as the key to an entire book or chapter and used as the text in the exposition of the whole. For example, the twentieth verse of the fourth chapter of Ephesians will provide a good text upon which to base an exposition of the entire chapter.

According to Purpose

We have seen how sermons may be divided into two classes according to their *style*. According to *purpose* they may be grouped into three classifications:

Doctrinal sermons. The purpose of this type of message is to set forth what the Bible teaches in regard to a doctrine. It is, therefore, definitely didactic in purpose. Such a message is bound, of course, to be expository in its style.

There is a definite need for preaching of this type. If the Christian is to give a reason for the hope that is within him, he must know the Word of God, must know what the Scripture teaches in regard to the great doctrines—the doctrines of regeneration, resurrection, heaven, the virgin birth, the deity of Christ, the trinity, etc. Thorough grounding in the doctrines of Scripture is the best assurance any minister can give his flock against emotional depression and spiritual declension. The wise preacher will bear in mind, however, that the teaching of doctrine is likely to be more beneficial to the Christian than to the sinner. Although by learning something of the great doctrines of the Bible, a sinner may come to a realization of his own state before God and of God's provision for his salvation, all the knowledge in the world about matters of doctrine will not be of profit to him unless his heart is touched and he is moved to a surrender to Christ. A wise pastor will not confine himself to doctrinal preaching, but will intersperse frequently simple Gospel messages addressed to the unsaved.

The doctrinal preacher should bear in mind, also, that great truths must be set forth in language simple enough to be understood by the layman untrained in theology if they are to be profitable to his congregation. It is dangerous, also, to take new Christians—"babes in Christ"—too rapidly into deep truths. Unless he is speaking to a congregation accustomed to doctrinal preaching and well taught in Scriptural truths, the preacher will do well to confine himself to the simple "milk of the Word."

In dealing with a doctrine, furthermore, the conscientious preacher will seek to ascertain what the Book teaches on the subject and will present that truth to his congregation. Doctrinal messages which seek to prove from the Scripture the preconceived ideas and opinions of the preacher or to stress a peculiar denominational interpretation by avoiding certain verses and overemphasizing others is not honest preaching.

Inspirational sermons. The *inspirational message,* which is generally a *thought sermon* in type, has as its purpose the stimulation and comfort of Christians—encouraging them to new service and inspiring them with greater zeal for the Lord's work. This type of sermon is particularly suitable to Christian young people's groups or commencement Sunday, New Year's day, etc., but it is always an effective message when delivered to Christian people. The *inspirational sermon* may, by setting forth a parallel between the difficulties and trials of some Bible character and those of the congregation, and showing how he overcame his, inspire the congregation to new courage and endeavor for the Lord. It may by showing the power of God inspire the hearers to new faith. It may by emphasizing their blessings create a new sense of content and trust in the providing hand of God. Again, by showing the need of the world the *inspirational sermon* may stimulate the Christian to new surrender and dedication and to the task of giving men the Gospel. This type of sermon has a necessary and important place in our ministry. All the "head knowledge" of doctrine in the world leaves a man cold and useless unless his heart is fired. There is danger in too much teaching without an accompanying heart enkindling. "Knowledge puffeth up," even Scriptural knowledge, unless accompanied by the warming emotion of love that edifieth. The answer to the problem of dead orthodoxy and spiritual lethargy in well-taught Christians will be found in inspirational preaching fired by the power of God's Holy Spirit.

Evangelistic sermons. The *evangelistic sermon* has as its primary purpose the conversion of sinners, though it seeks, also, to renew the zeal of the saints. It is the evangelistic message which has been generally used of God in bringing a spirit of revival. The prophets of the Old Testament were the evangelists of their day. The ministry of the apostles was to a great extent an evangelistic ministry. The missionary who bears fruit for the Lord is a missionary who is primarily evangelistic in his style and outlook. Nothing else will take the place of this type ministry. There has been a tendency in the last few years to discount the evangelist. Because ecclesiasticism cannot control and direct him, ecclesiasticism has sought to discredit or ignore him, but the gift of the evangelist is as definitely of God as the gift of the pastor or the teacher. While some men are particularly called of God to an evangelistic ministry, no preacher should neglect altogether this type of preaching. Indeed, every sermon should have an evangelistic note. If the chief duty of the preacher is the proclamation of the Gospel, it is wrong to push the evangelistic sermon with its Gospel emphasis into the background. A ministry that is fruitful in the salvation of souls will be a ministry with a definite evangelistic emphasis.

We grant that these systems of sermon classification are not wholly satisfactory, but we feel they are as nearly satisfactory as any classifications can be, and they have the decided advantage of simplicity. It is difficult to put any sermon arbitrarily into one of two groups as to its *style* or into one of three groups as to its *purpose*. The better a sermon the less likely it is to fit entirely into one classification, either in *style* or *purpose*. However, for convenience in study and analysis, sermons may be roughly classified as herein set forth.

III

TEXTS

THE PREACHER who accepts the doctrine of the inspiration of the Scripture and believes in the authority of the Book, will quite naturally turn to the Bible for the basis and foundation of his message. Voltaire expressed a wish that the practice of taking texts be abandoned. Some "popular" preachers of our day are following Voltaire's suggestion in this particular as they are following his materialistic philosophy in their sermonic teaching. It is an interesting commentary on their ministry that on so important a point as the abandoning of a Scriptural text they should be meeting the approval of the notorious eighteenth-century atheist, and the custom of speaking from a pulpit without taking a text from the Bible has developed apace with the "modernism" and so-called liberalism of our day.

"The custom of founding religious discourse upon a text, has prevailed ever since there has been a body of inspiration from which to take a text. In the patriarchal age, religious teachers spoke as they were moved by the Holy Ghost, without a passage from the Canon of inspiration, because the Canon was not yet formed. Noah was a 'preacher of righteousness,' and probably reasoned of righteousness, temperance, and judgment to come, much as Paul did before Felix, without any formal proposition derived from a body of Holy Writ. As early as the time of Ezra, however, we find the Sacred Canon, which during the captivity had fallen into neglect, made the basis of religious instruction. Ezra, accompanied by the Levites, in a public congregation, 'read in the law of God distinctly, and gave the sense, and caused them to understand the reading' (Nehemiah 8: 6-8). Our Saviour, as His custom was (conforming, undoubtedly, to the general Jewish custom), went into the synagogue on the Sabbath day, and 'stood up for to read' the Old Testament. He selected the first and part of the second verse of the sixty-first chapter of Isaiah for His text, and preached a sermon upon it, which fastened the eyes of every man in the synagogue upon Him, in the very beginning, and which, notwithstanding its gracious words, finally developed their latent malignity, and filled them with wrath, so that they led Him to the brow of the precipice on which their city was built, that they might cast Him down headlong [Luke 4: 16-29]. The apostles, also, frequently discoursed from passages of Scripture. Peter, soon after the return of the disciples from the Mount of Ascension, preached a discourse from Psalm 109: 8, the object of which was to induce the Church to choose an apostle in the place of Judas [Acts 1: 15]. And again, on the day of Pentecost, this same apostle preached a discourse, founded upon Joel 2: 28-32, which was instrumental in the conversion of three thousand souls. Sometimes, again, the discourse, instead of being more properly homiletic, was an abstract of sacred history. The discourse of Stephen, when arraigned before the high priest, was of this kind [Acts 7: 2-53]. The dense [sic] and mighty oration of Paul on Mars Hill, if examined, will be found to be made up, in no small degree, of statements and phrases that imply a thorough acquaintance with the Old Testament." *

There have been times in the history of the Christian church when, on account of the corruption of the canon, sermons were preached without texts. Some of the early church fathers followed this method, among them being Chrysostom and Augustine, the latter preaching over four hundred sermons without texts, but since the time of the Reformation up to the rapid development of "modernism," almost in our own generation, it has been customary to base a pulpit discourse on a portion of the Word of God.

It is the duty of the minister to "preach the Word," and a sermon should be founded upon or should be an interpretation of a portion of Scripture. The use of a text gives authority to the message. If the preacher interprets correctly the text which he chooses, his message is not his own idle speculation but the truth of God. The use of a text puts the preacher in his true relation to the people of his congregation and to his Lord. "I will put my words in thy mouth," said God to Jeremiah. It is the Word of God that the preacher is called upon to utter. A God-called preacher is a minister of God, speaking the Word of God, opening up God's thoughts, speaking for God. The Bible is vital and alive, different from all other literature. The inspired language impresses itself in the memory. It is the Word of God that carries the promise of divine blessing. Every sermon should be founded definitely upon it.

It goes without saying that the text should not be the only portion of the sermon in which the preacher quotes the Bible. The message should be filled with Scripture, and there

* William G. T. Shedd, *Homiletics and Pastoral Theology* (New York: Charles Scribner's Sons, 1867), pp. 160-62.

24

may be some sermons in which no single text is chosen but in which the discourse is based upon a whole passage. It is often best, however, to have a definite single text from the Scripture.

The text may be used to introduce the subject of the discourse. Sometimes, in fact, the text is itself the subject, and the mere statement of a well-chosen text may awaken the interest of the congregation in the subject with which the preacher proposes to deal. But the text does more than this. It will not only suggest the subject, but it will also in itself lend unity to the message. The text suggests a line of thought. The interpretation and exposition of the text is the exploration and development of that line of thought. Thus, a text not only presents the preacher with a line of thought to develop, but the text in itself may afford a logical means of developing it.

Phelps suggests a reason for using a text which might not readily occur to mind. It is a reason which, because of the growing tendency to discredit the Scripture, carries even more weight now than it did at the time of his writing (1892). Texts should be used, he suggests, in order

"to cherish in the minds of the hearers an attachment to the language of the Bible. In the popular notion of religious truth, words very easily become things. Never is language more readily consolidated into a living thing around which the reverence of a people will grow than when that language is long used to express their religious convictions, or their religious inheritance from their fathers. Therefore, if reverence be not cherished for the Scriptural forms of truth, it will be for uninspired forms. The popular mind will have it for something. We are suffering to-day from a morbid attachment, in some sections of the church, to uninspired standards of religious thought. A reverence is cherished for technicalities of theological science, and for certain forms of truth expressed in ritual and liturgic service, which nothing should receive but an inspired production. It has been believed by more than one of the lovers of the Book of Common Prayer that its authors and compilers were under the guidance of inspiration in their work. Views of divine superintendence have been advanced in behalf of the Westminster Confession which involve a subordinate degree of the inspired gifts in the leaders of the Westminster Assembly. Similar ideas have been expressed concerning the works of John Wesley. A very intelligent Baptist clergyman once inquired of me if I did not believe that something very like apostolic inspiration was imparted to Robert Hall." *

There are several things to be considered in choosing a text. First of all, the preacher is faced with the necessity of selecting a text which appeals to him personally. It is doubtful that a great sermon can be preached from a text which does not interest and grip the preacher. A text which stirs the imagination and excites his interest, it is safe to assume, will, if he has any gifts for preaching, provide him with a sermon which will stimulate and convict the hearers. But there are other considerations to be borne in mind in the selection of a text. Among them are these: What is the need of the congregation to whom the sermon is to be preached? For what type congregation is the message intended? Will it be for the most part made up of Christians or sinners? Will it be delivered to a young people's group or to older people, or to a group of varying ages? All these will influence the preacher in the selection of his text.

Many authorities on the subject of homiletics see fit to establish definite methods of determining what constitutes good and bad texts. While some verses offer more opportunities than others, most portions of the Word of God may be used as texts and if properly handled there seems no good reason to avoid them. Of course, the minister should bear in mind that certain passages in the King James version do not accurately express the meaning of the original language and that there are some verses interpolated in the English

* Austin Phelps, *The Theory of Preaching*. (New York: Charles Scribner's Sons, 1892), p. 56.

version which are not found in the earliest manuscripts. It is well to remember, also that while the Bible in the original language is a verbally inspired record all the thoughts set down in the Scripture are not inspired thoughts. The record is accurate, but the words and thoughts of men accurately set down are not always true. For example, the book of Ecclesiastes is the record of a man's thoughts and philosophical reasoning. This book is not intended to give us God's view of man's life, but rather a man's own reasoning about life. Accurately set down in the inspired record are the false words of wicked men—of Cain, and of Saul, and of Judas, and many others. Also recounted is the false reasoning of good men—the arguments of Job and his friends, for example. Even Satan is quoted, and we are told he is "the father of lies." Therefore, while the Scripture is inspired, everything said in the Word of God is not true, for the errors of man as he seeks to reason things out for himself and the lying words of Satan are included. If such a passage is chosen for a text, and such a passage may sometimes make a good text, the preacher must in his interpretation of the text bear in mind that while the record is inspired, the sentiments may not be. Such texts should never be used to prove a doctrine. The words of men quoted in the Scripture are often in contradiction of each other and of the plain teaching of the Holy Spirit.

Therefore, before developing a text, it is wise for the preacher to ask himself these questions: First, who wrote the book of which the text is a part? Under what circumstances was it written? For what purpose? To whom? If the text is a quotation, who is quoted? Why was the statement made? Is it true? A portion of Scripture can never be considered apart from its context, even though it is selected as the text for a *thought sermon*, and the preacher should give some attention (generally in his introduction) to the circumstances attending the text and to its context.

As a general rule, a short text is better than a long one. The hearer is more apt to remember the text if it consists of one single clear-cut statement. The text may be a portion of a verse. Usually the text should be a complete grammatical sentence, but bits of a phrase are sometimes more arresting. Spurgeon preached a sermon for which his text was, "If thou be the Son of God" (Matthew 4:3), the first word of the text being the point of emphasis in the message. Certain Biblical fragments such as this afford great textual possibilities. Others offering good opportunities to the preacher are numerous. Here are two good examples: "If I will" (John 21:22), "In remembrance of me" (Luke 22:19). It is a wise preacher who fits the text to the needs of his subjects and who remembers that usually the text should not set forth more facts than the sermon discusses.

Sometimes a minister may very wisely select two or more texts for the same sermon, but this should not be done simply to add dignity to his subject by an accumulation of Scriptural references. The body of the message is the proper place to add other evidence from the Scripture in support of its interpretation or argument. When the sermon treats one subject, one text is enough to introduce it. Parallel texts may be chosen where there are parallel subjects to be discussed or where one subject is to be treated in various aspects, in which case a text may be selected as a basis for the discussion of each aspect of the subject. For example, in discussing the purpose of Christ in His incarnation as contrasted with the purpose of His second advent, one might effectively use such parallel texts as these, "Behold the Lamb of God, which taketh away the sin of the world" (John 1:29), and "The Lord God omnipotent reigneth" (Revelation 19:6).

Multiple texts are generally chosen only for sermons in which comparisons are to be made and contrasts are to be drawn. Spurgeon chose this pair of texts for one of his sermons: Mark 5:16, "But when he saw Jesus afar off, he ran and worshiped him"; and Luke 15:20: "And he arose, and came to his father, but when he was yet a great way off, his father saw him, and had compassion, and ran, and fell on his neck, and kissed him." I cannot help feeling, however, that the sermon based upon them was not one of Spurgeon's best efforts. The point of parallel of the message was that while afar off the sinner saw the Saviour, and while afar off the father saw the prodigal. A more definite parallelism is to be preferred in the selection of multiple texts.

The preacher should beware of choosing a text which promises more than the sermon delivers. A lofty text demands a lofty sermon. Such texts as Revelation 19:15, "And out of his mouth goeth a sharp sword, that with it he should smite the nations. He shall rule them with a rod of iron; and he treadeth the winepress of the fierceness and wrath of Almighty God" will lead a congregation to anticipate an unusual discourse. If such a text is chosen, however, it is possibly better to announce it after the introduction has warmed the speaker and the audience up to the dramatic level of the text itself, for after the declaration of such a text, it is rather difficult to begin a sermon on the quiet conversational level which gives the audience an opportunity to become warmed up to the preacher's level of interest. Grand and lofty texts should not be altogether avoided. They are particularly good to use on special occasions—but the preacher who overuses such texts is liable to come to the place where he strains after effect instead of preaching for results. His sermons will then become "full of sound and fury, signifying nothing."

While it is true that one can never exhaust the Word of God, it is also true that some texts have been used so often that the listener hearing them announced, sighs to himself and thinks, "I shall hear the same old sermon again," and, as a matter of fact, certain passages have been so often preached upon that it is almost impossible to treat them in any original way. It would take a great preacher, for example, to find a fresh treatment of the text, "Wherefore seeing we also are compassed about with so great a cloud of witnesses, let us lay aside every weight, and the sin which doth so easily beset us, and let us run with patience the race that is set before us" (Hebrews 12:1). This verse, admittedly one of the great texts of the Bible, has been so thoroughly treated that among average churchgoers there will not be an individual who has not heard a number of sermons upon it.

It is often wise to avoid a text that is too obvious in its implications. It was no compliment to the intuition, tact, or imagination of the various preachers who Sunday after Sunday had conducted services in a certain prison that it was finally necessary to display this sign where the gaze of the preacher as he ascended the pulpit must certainly fall upon it: "Don't preach on the prodigal son!"

It is to be recommended that a preacher study the Bible with the idea of finding unhackneyed texts, and there is no harm occasionally in a congregation's hearing such an unusual text announced that it wonders what the preacher can possibly say about it. While novelty is not the most important element to consider in the selection of a text, the audience interest which such a text stimulates will be a help to the preacher in driving home the truth. Novel texts make for variety in preaching. They stimulate the listeners to remember the sermon because of the text, and they stimulate the preacher himself in the preparation of the message.

No preacher should confine himself, however, to novel texts. Sometimes an old and familiar text affords opportunities for not one but a series of effective messages such as that group of sermons preached by Harry Moorehouse from John 3:16, which made so profound an impression on Dwight L. Moody. Some unusual and some familiar texts should be chosen by every minister, but in the development of the familiar text he should cultivate originality of treatment.

Even obscure texts, however, have certain advantages. The exposition of an obscure verse will increase the congregation's knowledge of the Word of God, and obscure texts, like unusual and novel texts, tend to interest the hearer. They are technically useful to the preacher, since they do not immediately suggest the subject of the sermon and, therefore, enable the preacher to introduce it subtly—a procedure which is psychologically advisable when dealing with a subject against which the audience has a prejudice. Obscure texts should always be interpreted in the light of clear texts, and sermons which are intended to teach a doctrine should not be based upon an obscure text.

The text of a sermon and the theme of a sermon should be congruent. A text should never be chosen which does not contain the subject, either directly, by implication, or by suggestion; and a text which is unrelated to the subject of the sermon in one of these three ways is not a text at all. The ideal text will express exactly the theme of the sermon and no more, and a text should not set forth a different aspect of the subject from that with which the sermon undertakes to deal. A general text should not be chosen for a sermon which deals with some specific aspect of the subject suggested by the text, and the text should be suitable in style to the type message preached from it.

In the selection of his text, as in his development of it, the minister should always remember that he is dealing with the Word of God—divine, holy, God-breathed. It should be handled with the respect and reverence which is its due. The Scripture should never be made the subject of a jest or used for the purpose of humor in a story, and should never be lightly treated. "The Word of God is quick and powerful and sharper than a two-edged sword," and it should be handled as carefully as a keen weapon. The minister of God both in selecting a portion of the Word for use as his text and in developing it should always seek the leading of the Holy Spirit.

IV

AN ANALYSIS OF
SERMON CONSTRUCTION

THERE ARE THREE main divisions to every sermon: the
introduction, the body, and the conclusion. Each part is
important.

THE INTRODUCTION

The introduction serves more than one purpose. In the
first place, it gives the audience an opportunity to become
acquainted with the speaker. When a man stands before a
familiar congregation, made up of those who have heard him
frequently, this office of the introduction is not so important. However, when the preacher is new to the congregation, when he stands before them for the first time, it is
essential that they be afforded an opportunity to accustom
themselves somewhat to his voice and to his manner of
speech. Even from his own pulpit, the preacher will frequently see strangers in his congregation and in a down-
town church he may expect visitors every Sunday. The
introduction serves a valuable purpose in permitting them
to become accustomed to the preacher so that they will be
able to concentrate upon the message. By the time the introduction is over the preacher himself should be forgotten
and the hearers should be occupied with the sermon. The
introduction, then, introduces the preacher to the congregation.

It is customary for a visiting speaker to be presented to
an audience. This presentation is sometimes called an introduction and the person making it often concludes by saying, "I am very happy to introduce to you Rev. Mr. ———."
Actually, he *presents* him. A congregation does not really
become acquainted with a speaker until after he begins to
speak. His introduction should, therefore, introduce him to

them, but this does not mean that it should contain any personal reference. When a minister has been presented to a congregation, it is customary for him to say a few words of acknowledgment and then express his pleasure at being present. From these words he may move into the introduction of his message without any noticeable break or with only a slight pause between the two. He should never convey the idea, "Now, since that preliminary is over, I shall begin to preach." Even following the words which common courtesy and pulpit amenities demand from a new or visiting minister, the introduction to the sermon itself will still serve to accustom the audience to the speaker, since the preliminary words of greeting are rarely of sufficient length to accomplish this fully.

The second purpose of the introduction is to introduce the subject of the message. The title may be known to the congregation because they have heard it announced or seen it printed in the bulletin, but as is pointed out elsewhere, the title and the subject of the sermon are not always the same. The introduction must make the audience aware of the theme which the preacher intends to discuss. It is best that this not be done bluntly, and it is not generally wise to reveal the subject too early in the introduction. It is poor psychology to begin the sermon by saying, "I propose to talk to you today about such-and-such a subject," or "The theme of my sermon this morning is to be so-and-so." Actually there may not be anywhere a definite statement of the subject as such, but by the time the introduction is over the audience should know the theme of the sermon.

The text is generally announced in the introduction. The wise preacher, however, will employ variety in the method and place of introduction. Under rare circumstances indeed should it be bluntly quoted or introduced simply with the words, "My text this morning is ——." Generally, the text comes near the beginning of the introduction. Sometimes, however, it should go at the very end of it. The choice of procedure employed in introducing the text will depend to some extent upon the type of sermon to be delivered upon it.

Occasionally matters of great local or national interest can be referred to in connection with the announcement of the text. On the Sunday after the news had arrived in the New England Colonies that the Stamp Act had been repealed, a pastor in Boston attracted his hearers' attention by tying this news to his text by these words, "Were I to serve you in the ministry of the Gospel for a century I might never again have so favorable an opportunity to address you upon these words, 'As cold waters to a thirsty soul, so is good news from a far country.'"

The introduction may, in the third place, set the stage for the discussion which is to follow. If a text consists of words spoken by an individual on a certain occasion, the audience should be acquainted with the circumstances attending the utterance of the words. The introduction may relate the text to the context, though this is sometimes done in the body of the discourse. The introduction should make the audience know what kind of sermon to expect. It should in its form and literary style be similar to the rest of the sermon. A solemn sermon needs a solemn introduction; an inspirational message does not. If the sermon is to be an expository sermon, the introduction should suggest this. However, the preacher should bear in mind that his introduction, while suggesting the message which is to follow and resembling it as a part of the same rhetorical structure, should accomplish the other purposes as well.

A good introduction will do more than introduce the preacher and the subject and give the setting of the message. It will do more than give the congregation an opportunity to forget the preacher, having become accustomed to him, and concentrate upon the message. It will prepare the minds of the congregation for the reception and digestion of it. It will attract the attention of the audience and arouse their interest. It will prepare them to agree with what the preacher will say. The preacher's mind by reason of thought and preparation will be already focused upon the subject of his sermon. The introduction should bring his hearers as nearly as possible to his own level of interest.

It is particularly important that any public speaker gain the attention of his hearers at the very beginning of his address. It is well to remember that you "get" your hearers in the first three minutes or you are not likely to "get" them at all—certainly not in time for the message to do them much good. With the possible exception of the final climax, no part of the sermon is more important than its opening paragraphs. The first minute should establish between speaker and audience a feeling of interest and understanding.

It is wise particularly in speaking to a strange audience to make the first minute "disarming." It is necessary to cultivate tact and charm if this is to be accomplished. One may go so far as to leave no particular impression of skill and ability as a speaker, but if one accomplishes his purpose in this first minute it is evidence not only of speech skill but also of cleverness and good judgment. This first minute is particularly important in dealing with certain type audiences, audiences which are normally suspicious of a preacher —if not openly hostile to the Gospel—, for example, high school assemblies, professional groups, clubs, and fraternal organizations. When a preacher is presented, some such audiences throw up a psychological barrier—"He is up to something"; "We do not want to be preached to"; "We are in for a dull and tiresome twenty minutes"; "We had better watch this fellow to be sure he does not put something over on us."

An example of tact in disarming an audience was demonstrated by a chaplain from Massachusetts who was preaching to a wealthy Presbyterian congregation while the Northern army was in possession of the city of Norfolk during the Civil War. The Northern preacher was in the pulpit upon the command of his general, and the Confederates were in the pews in obedience to military orders. The preacher began the sermon with these words, "My friends, I am here by no choice of mine. I came to your city as a chaplain, to look after the souls of my neighbors who are here, as I am, under military rule. I stand in the place of your honored pastor by command of my military superior; but I am a preacher of the same Christ whom you possess, and I ask you to hear me for His sake." All other things being equal, the preacher who accomplishes the most in the time allotted for his message will be the preacher who best overcomes a hostile feeling on the part of his hearers in the first minute or minute and a half of speaking.

Cicero said that the purposes of the introduction are to "render the hearers kindly disposed, attentive, teachable." Having rendered them kindly disposed toward the speaker and toward his subject, the speaker should during the next several minutes by strong composition and excellency of delivery proceed to stimulate the interest of his audience— "render them attentive."

A bit of narrative or an appropriate illustration may be employed to great advantage. There is no place in a message where the dramatization of ideas can accomplish more than in the introduction. There is no place where the use of suggestiveness and imagination can be more effective. For example, the introduction to a sermon based on Christ's conversation with Peter as recorded in the last chapter of John may effectively begin with this sentence, "The mists of early morning veiled the shadowy figure standing beside the flickering embers on the beach." Sometimes, however, the most dramatic sentence is the simplest sentence, a simple fact simply stated. And for many a preacher that which is most simply said is most effectively said.

Sunday after Sunday, churchgoers hear a sermon. The preacher must discuss themes on which many of them have heard a number of sermons. He should handle these themes in such a new fashion that their interest will be aroused afresh. Some preachers attempt to overcome this disadvantage of the frequency of preaching by sensationalism in preaching. Others—of course, among the liberals—have substituted other types of speeches for sermons. However, whatever disadvantage the preacher may face from dealing with familiar themes is more than compensated for by the constant freshness of the Word of God and by the power of the Gospel. But the wise preacher will seek in his introduction to attract the attention of his hearers to a familiar theme by a fresh approach and by originality of style. He will not stoop to the sensational nor depart from the practice of preaching.

There will be rare occasions when the audience does not need to be aroused and interested. Such an occasion was the funeral of Louis XIV. Massillon entered the pulpit, looked down at the coffin of the king, stood for a moment with sad countenance, then looked into the face of the assembled nobility of France and uttered this simple word of introduction, "My brethren, only God is great." No further introduction was necessary.

Circumstances alter the introduction and the same introduction is not always advisable for the same message. The Sunday after a nation has declared war a congregation will expect the words of the minister to be effected by this fact. Any great tragedy or calamity which has made a profound impression upon the people will shape somewhat the construction of the introduction of a sermon. A preacher should be psychologist enough to relate his message to such moods on the part of his congregation. The minds of his hearers are occupied with some great common thought. Instead of trying to turn their minds from that thought abruptly to his message, he will by means of his introduction tie his message in with their thought. He will not turn them abruptly to his subject. He will lead them to it gradually along the direction which their thought is taking. When a community has been stirred by some deep emotion he will shape the mood of his introduction into its mold. St. Chrysostom standing before a congregation which had just gone through the frightening experience of a great earthquake began a sermon with these words: "Do you see the power of God? Do you see the benignity of God? His power, because the solid world He has shaken; His benignity, because the falling world He has supported."

A good introduction prepares the heart of the hearer for the truths which the preacher will utter—"render them," in the words of Cicero, "teachable." The preacher in Goldsmith's "The Deserted Village" must have been a master of the art of the introduction. His hearers "came to scoff, remained to pray." Paul at Mar's Hill magnificently accomplished this purpose in his introduction. In a city where the preaching of a new religion and the introduction of a new god was a capital crime, Paul, though his spirit burned within him, tactfully said, "I perceive that you are very religious. I find among you an altar to the 'unknown god.' I should like to talk to you about him." * He found what was apparently a common point between the interest of his audience and the subject of his sermon and used that in introducing his message. This was good homiletics. It was also good psychology.

THE BODY

The body of the sermon expounds the text, develops the thesis, or presents the argument. To be effectively presented, the material contained should be well organized, and, therefore, developed according to a carefully prepared outline. Such an outline may contain as many points as necessary for the development of the sermon. Medieval theologians held that an orthodox sermon must have three points. But they were not the only ones who have held a high regard for this number. Phelps writing in the late nineteenth century said,

* Acts 17: 22-23: "Then Paul stood in the midst of Mars' hill, and said, Ye men of Athens, I perceive that in all things ye are too superstitious [i.e. very religious]. For as I passed by, and beheld your devotions, I found an altar with this inscription, TO THE UNKNOWN GOD. Whom therefore ye ignorantly worship, him declare I unto you."

"I once heard a sermon before an association of clergymen approved for consisting of three general divisions, each of which had three subdivisions, each of these being developed with three leading thoughts, and all followed by three inferences in the conclusion, and ending with the Trinitarian Doxology. The preacher should have delivered it in a three-cornered hat. Such a discourse is a miserable piece of trichotomy. The taste which could delight in it is like that which enjoys anagrams and acrostics. Persuasive speech is infinitely above it." *

While we agree with Phelps that this is rather "running things into the ground," we feel that psychologically it is not a bad principle to limit one's outline to three main points when the material can be effectively covered within the limits of this number, since the fewer the points brought out the more apt the congregation will be to retain them and to follow the preacher as he develops them. However, if it takes more than three points to develop the message, use them. In treating the average subject it would perhaps be wiser to limit the scope of the message to that which can be covered in a few points and develop those few well than to attempt to develop a great many points briefly and incompletely. William Jay commonly used five points for his outline. Spurgeon was not so consistent. Generally, however, he confined himself to not more than four, sometimes to three, and quite often to two.

As the preacher begins the discussion of the body of his message, passing into it from his introduction, there is no reason why the listener should be too emphatically aware of his passage from the one to the other. Some preachers, as they leave the introduction, give the impression of one who, having passed out of one room into another, slams the door noisily behind him. In a well-organized message each portion will flow naturally into the other. Though in studying

* Austin Phelps, *The Theory of Preaching*. (New York: Charles Scribner's Sons, 1892), p. 383.

the outline or reading the sermon in manuscript one can discover the various portions and determine where each ends and the next begins, there is no reason for such transitions to be obvious in the delivery of the message. It is not advisable, as a general thing, to make the progression from point to point in the main body of the sermon too apparent, except in the case of the doctrinal message, where the preacher is seeking to impress each point into the minds of the hearers that they may retain the outline for their own further study of and meditation upon the doctrine which he is teaching.

In the development of the body of the message itself there should be definite progression. That is to say, the simplest and least complicated or least important points should be made first and the others so in order of their relative importance that the last point is the strongest of all.

It is a good rule never to introduce any point of the outline until one has come to the place in the outline where he intends to develop it. It is poor psychology to let the congregation know at the beginning of the message the points that the speaker intends to discuss. While such a method is excellent for a lawyer in trying a case before a jury and is recommended for a debater seeking to win a decision from the judges, it is poor technique for a preacher. There can be little reason for the idea some preachers seem to have that they should actually preach a sermon three times—first, tell the congregation what they are going to say, then say it, and finally tell them what they said. About the only good thing that can be said about this is that such reiteration may fix the facts in the minds of those who listen to such a repetitious discourse. Such a method has decided disadvantages. Some of the congregation, when they hear the preacher say in the beginning of his message under what points he plans to develop his text, will think, "He is going to prove his points for those three or four reasons. Well, I know what he is going to talk about, so why should I bother to listen?" The preacher who somewhere toward the first of his message says, "We shall see this morning that this fact is true for three reasons," which he then proceeds to name over, fails to take advantage of the suspense element as a means of holding attention. Announce the point when you plan to develop it. Better still, if possible, develop the point without ever making a blunt announcement of it. Introduce it more subtly.

The outline is merely the skeleton of the message. Though the points be well arranged and logically placed, they do not constitute a sermon. They are simply the foundation upon which the sermon itself is to be built. They are naked and bare until they are clothed with the supporting material which make up the sermon. Such material may be considered as consisting of five different types.

First, there is *explanation*. This form of support, though essential and necessary, is rarely sufficient and adequate in itself and it oftentimes contains some of the other forms of supporting material. This is factual, definitive material which makes clear the meaning of the terms which the preacher is using, or explains definitely what he has in mind.

The second type of supporting material is *comparison* and *analogy*. Dr. Jowett gives a good example of the use of this type of material in his sermon "The Abiding Companionship":

"Well, here we are facing the unknown road of the New Year. Where is the road going to lead? We do not know; we are alike in the common ignorance; culture and wealth can play no favorites; all distinctions are here wiped out; we are all upon an unknown road and for everybody the next step is in the mist. The knowledge of the future path matters nothing; the perception of the present companionship matters everything, and so our motto entwines the gracious offer of a companionship for the unknown and changing road."

Analogy and comparison, it will be seen from the above illustration, mean the pointing out of similarities between that which is known and that which is unknown or between the concrete and the abstract. A good example of the use of this type material is afforded by the comparison of salvation to a ship, and who has not heard a sermon preached on "The Old Ship of Zion," in which this comparison was drawn fully and completely throughout the entire message?

The third type of supporting material is *illustration*, which may be of three sorts, factual, hypothetical, or a specific instance. A factual illustration is, as the term indicates, a narrative presenting actual facts to illuminate the thought expressed. A good example of a factual illustration and its application is afforded by C. F. Butterfield:

"When Munkacsy's picture 'Christ before Pilate,' was on exhibition in the lower part of Canada, a rough-looking man came to the door of the tent and said, 'Is Jesus Christ here?' When informed that the picture was there, he asked the price of admission. Throwing down a piece of silver, he passed in and stood in the presence of the masterpiece. He kept his hat on, sat down on the chair before the painting and brushed off the catalogue. The one having the picture in charge had a desire to see how such a picture would move such a man. The man sat for a moment, and then reverently removed his hat, stooped and picked up the catalogue, and looked first at it, and then at that marvelous face, while tears rolled down his cheeks. He sat there for an hour, and when he left, he said: 'I am a rough sailor from the lakes, but I promised my mother before I went on this last cruise that I would go and see Jesus Christ. I never believed in such things before, but a man who could paint a picture like that must believe in the man, and he makes me believe in him, too.' It is a marvelous thing that there is power in a canvas, when touched by a master hand to save a soul. It is also marvelous that your life and mine may be so transformed that people can see in us Jesus Christ."

A hypothetical illustration is narrative which *could have happened* or *perhaps will happen*. William Gurnall, who made such excellent use of illustrative material, in his classic,

"The Christian in Complete Armor," uses and applies a hypothetical illustration in the following way:

"Suppose a king's son should get out of a besieged city where he hath left his wife and children, whom he loves as his own soul, and these all ready to die by sword or famine, if supply come not the sooner. Could this prince, when arrived at his father's house, please himself with the delights of the court and forget the distress of his family? or rather would he not come post to his father, having their cries and groans always in his ears, and before he ate or drank do his errand to his father, and entreat him if he ever loved him that he would send all the force of his kingdom to raise the siege rather than any of his dear relations should perish? Surely, sirs, though Christ be in the top of his preferment and out of the storm in regard of his own person, yet his children, left behind in the midst of sin's, Satan's, and the world's batteries, are in his heart, and shall not be forgotten a moment by him. The care he takes in our business appeared in the speedy dispatch he made of his spirit to his apostles' supply, which, as soon almost as he was warm in his seat at his Father's right hand, he sent, to the incomparable comfort of his apostles and us that to this day— yea, to the end of the world—do or shall believe on him."

The specific instance is actually a factual illustration without details. The limitations of time may prevent a preacher from using more than one detailed example or illustration to clarify or strengthen his argument. In such cases specific instances may be included. In an Easter message James Learmount uses two such instances consecutively:

"The grave of Albert Dürer, the great painter, is in the cemetery of his native city, Nuremburg, in Germany; on his tombstone they have put the word *Emigravit*—he has emigrated, gone to another country. That is the truth. Nothing can die that is related to Jesus, He is the Lord of life.

"The early Christians knew that. Over one of the burying places in the catacombs of Rome there is an epitaph which says: *Tentianus vivit*, that is, 'Tentianus lives.'"

The next type of material is one which is not often adapted to sermonic construction but which will be occasionally found useful. It is *statistical material*. Statistics are forceful proof when effectively used, but should be made clear and understandable to the listeners. Nowhere is the use of dramatization of ideas so important as in dealing with statistics.

The last and most important form of support which may be used in developing the points of a sermon is *testimony*. In a sermon this will consist largely of quotation from the Bible giving testimony from God Himself of the truth which the preacher is setting forth, or proof from the testimony of Bible characters that in their own experience such facts have proved true. Naturally, however, all testimony will not be confined to the Scripture, but the testimony of any men, living or dead, can be introduced. Such testimony is generally most effectively presented in the form of direct quotation.

THE CONCLUSION

The purpose of the conclusion is to tie together the threads of the sermon and to motivate the congregation to decision and action. It is an appeal for response. Having in the body of his message shown them that certain things are true, the preacher should in his conclusion challenge them to do something about it. Generally, there should be an appeal of salvation made to the sinner and a challenge to service to Christians. Though an invitation will not always be given following the message, the appeal should be so definite that some inward response will be motivated. Spurgeon's theory of the conclusion of a sermon was that it

"should end with the inculcation of some great, vital principle or some strong, majestic declaration of God—so that that principle or that declaration should be the highest peak of the range." *

* Arthur H. Smith, *Preachers and Preaching* (Philadelphia: The United Lutheran Publication House, 1925), p. 92.

44

It was in this fashion that he closed his sermons. Having finished, he would lift his hands impressively, often dramatically, and pronounce the benediction and send the people out, "with that principle or declaration on the very top of their minds."

The conclusion should be generally on a high and lofty plane but should be, also, a definite part of the message. The early church fathers were masters at the art of tying the conclusion in appropriately to the message. St. Chrysostom closed a sermon in this fashion: "For so shall we be able to pass the present life with happiness and obtain to the peace of heaven with Jesus Christ, to whom be glory and dominion together with the Father and the Holy Spirit, forever and ever, Amen!" This inclusion of a Gloria at the end of a sermon sometimes makes a most effective finish.

An excellent example of the conclusion as an integral part of the message is afforded in Basil's sermon on the creation of the world, in which he deals with the creation of light and the dispersion of darkness.

"But while I am conversing with you about the first evening of the world, evening takes me by surprise and puts an end to my discourse. May the Father of the true light, who has adorned day with celestial light, who has made to shine the fires which illuminate us during the night, who reserves for us in the peace of a future age a spiritual and everlasting light, enlighten your hearts in the knowledge of truth, keep you from stumbling, and grant that 'you may walk honestly as in the day.' Thus shall you shine as the sun in the midst of the glory of the saints, and I shall glory in you in the day of Christ, to whom belong all glory and power for ever and ever. Amen."

Though usually a conclusion will be somewhat more lengthy than this of Basil's, this is a conclusion that lends a graceful finish and actually includes an appropriate benediction as a part of the sermon itself.

There is no part of the sermon more important than the

conclusion. Even more than the introduction it deserves great thought and care in preparation. Upon the last few minutes of a message may rest the eternal destiny of a hearer, who in them may be brought to a position of surrender to Christ. In the last few minutes of a sermon, Christians may be moved to surrender and dedication of their lives and service. The language of the conclusion should be strong and forceful. The appeal should be direct and heart-searching. It is imperative, particularly in an evangelistic message, that each listener feel the preacher is speaking directly to him as he draws his message to a close. There is no other time where a direct audience contact is so important; there is no other place in the message where the preacher needs to exercise more skillfully his psychological bases of appeal. There is no place where there should be a more definite climactic progression both in the arrangement of material and in its presentation. Many an otherwise poor sermon has been redeemed by a strong introduction and a strong conclusion, and many a sermon which moved along nicely until its closing moments was ruined by a poor conclusion. It is a good idea to prepare the conclusion of the sermon in advance, and even to write it out fully. Too many sermons simply fade out at the end. The preacher has concentrated upon what he wished to say in his sermon and has given no thought as to how he could conclude the message; when he has finished what he had intended saying he is at a loss for a proper conclusion. Because the ending is weak, because he misses good stopping places or seems to be groping for one, his hearers forget the good impression which the message itself has made and take away with them the memory of the weak ending.

V

IMPROVING THE
LITERARY QUALITY OF A SERMON

IT IS NOT THE PURPOSE of this chapter to set forth certain arbitrary standards by which to measure the literary greatness of a sermon, but rather to suggest certain technical excellencies which should be developed by the preacher who wishes to improve the literary quality of his messages.

Preachers follow different methods in the construction and delivery of their sermons. Some men write out their sermons and deliver them from memory or read them from the manuscript. Others prepare outlines from which they speak without having definitely chosen in advance the exact phraseology they will use in the pulpit. Whichever method is followed, the sermon should possess certain elements of good literary style. By that is not meant that a sermon should possess the literary characteristics of a short story or novel or even of an essay. Not only is a sermon different from these in its literary type, but it is different also in its purpose. These are written to be read; sermons are preached to be heard. Sermons which greatly stirred their hearers as they fell from the lips of the preacher may leave one who reads them from the pages of a book altogether unmoved. Phillips Brooks was one of the great preachers of his day, yet a printed volume of his sermons is, to many people, notably unimpressive. It is wise in constructing a sermon to keep in mind that it is not intended primarily to live in print. It is intended at the moment of preaching to enter the minds and hearts of those who hear it. Literary immortality should not be sought after, although there are some men of exceptional gifts and background whose sermons as preached, and with almost no editing, possess permanent literary value. The results desired from a sermon are present, not future, and it is doubtful that any preacher who goes into the pulpit without a deep and earnest desire to secure immediate results secures any results at all. It is a rare sermon that the congregation remembers with any degree of clarity a week later.

By good literary style is meant, therefore, the rhetorical style which contributes most effectively to the accomplishment of the purpose for which a sermon is constructed. Among the important elements of such a style is *accuracy*.

The preacher should say exactly what he means and, it might be added, mean exactly what he says. It is a sad fact that many preachers are known to be exaggerators. A congregation of two hundred is referred to as a congregation of four hundred. Preachers have been known to refer to "the throng which poured into the building" when actually a few people had wandered in, one or two at a time—most of them late—all of whom scarcely filled the few back pews. Such statements are not merely inaccurate. They are false. In a literary sense inaccuracy means the use either of a word whose meaning is not precisely what is intended or a vagueness in regard to facts which should be clearly stated. The word does not imply complete or deliberate misrepresentation of fact.

To be accurate, one must not only think clearly but also possess a vocabulary broad enough so that from it he can cut a garment of words that fits properly his idea. For example, a storm may be either a snowstorm, a rainstorm, a hailstorm, a sandstorm, or a windstorm. In speaking of a storm, a preacher should be so specific in his choice of words that his hearers need not wonder what kind of storm he had in mind. An old man may be feeble, or doddering, or senile. His disposition may be petulant, querulous, irascible, testy, or disputatious; his voice harsh or piercing or hoarse or cracked. *Disagreeable* is an adjective that would describe his disposition and *unpleasant* an adjective that would describe his voice, but neither of these general words is as accurate as the specific adjective which applies most exactly to the disposition and voice of the particular old man under discussion.

48

Perhaps these may seem tedious and overnice differentiations. It is granted that such a technical use of words can be overdone, but it is not so likely that a preacher will become overtechnical in his choice of words as it is that he will be inaccurate.

Every preacher should possess either a good thesaurus of the English language or a good dictionary of synonyms and antonyms, which should not be allowed to grow dusty for lack of use. Out of many synonyms, there is sometimes just one which embodies the exact meaning the preacher wishes to convey. Any other word is a makeshift. Every man whose business involves the use of the English language from the public platform should use it as effectively as possible, and it goes without saying that every preacher should certainly be accurate enough not to confuse or interchange the meanings of such words as *accept* and *except, affect* and *effect, illusion* and *elusion, leave* and *let, lie* and *lay, rise* and *raise.*

Force. It is possible for a man to be forceful in his manner of delivery in the pulpit who is not forceful in the construction of his sermons; but the most forceful speaking will be greatly handicapped by a weak sermon. He is doubly effective as a preacher whose sermons are forcefully constructed as well as forcefully delivered. In forceful construction the material is so organized, arranged, and expressed that the sermon possesses a vitality which of itself demands attention, even if the sermon is not forcefully delivered.

A number of things go to make up a forceful sermonic style. The choice of strong words is important. Specific words are stronger than general words. The word *thing* should be avoided whenever possible and a specific word used. The tedious overuse of a specific word, however, can be just as bad as the use of a general word. *Cheating, lying, stealing* are stronger words than *dishonesty*. *Love for father and mother* has a stronger connotation than *filial affection*. *Rot* is a more forceful word than *decay*. Abused and overworked words and phases, such as *factor, item, along that line, awfully funny,* weaken the message.

Simple words are generally more forceful than unusual and uncommon words. Words of few syllables are often stronger than those of many syllables. Short sentences are often more forceful than long ones, and brief statements may strike more fire than lengthy discussion. Concise phrases, each complete in itself, piled the one upon the other, can be more forceful than paragraph added to lengthy paragraph.

Many a good sermon has been smothered by too heavy a blanket of words. If a preacher will write out his sermon and before preaching it go back and cut out unnecessary words and phrases, his literary style will benefit and so will his hearers. There is many a patient congregation that might earnestly pray: "From verbosity and tautology, good Lord, deliver us." Luther wisely said, "I would not have preachers torment their hearers, and detain them with long and tedious preaching, for the delight of hearing vanishes therewith, and the preachers hurt themselves." However, important ideas may be forcefully presented by the use of repetition, but the repetition should be of the idea and not of the words. That is, the same thought should be restated in different language. Parallel construction wisely used and not overworked makes for power and vitality.

Proper organization and arrangement of the ideas lend force to a sermon. As a general rule, the most important and climactic point should be set forth last, but there should be throughout the sermon a changing level of interest values. Each paragraph needs a climax and each section, made up as it is of a combination of paragraphs, needs a climactic paragraph. Usually the climax of the message is found toward the close. By skillful use of climaxes, the interest of the listener is held throughout the sermon. The weakness of anticlimactic construction is shown by the classic humorous example of the man who said to his enemy: "You have robbed me of my wealth, taken away my good name, wrecked my home, broken the heart of my wife—but don't go too far." DeQuincy affords this caricature, "If a man indulges himself in murder, he very soon comes to think little of robbery, and from robbing he comes to drinking and from that to incivility and procrastination."

Suggestiveness and imagination. It is sometimes better to suggest a line of thought than to explore it, wiser to sketch in the outline of a situation than to depict it in full detail. Artists make use of this psychological principle. The chief figure is high-lighted on the canvas while the details are indistinct or left to the imagination. In making a nation at war conscious of the danger of promiscuously discussing the movements of ships, nothing could be more effective than the poster showing underneath the simple words, "Somebody talked," a close view of a sailor's cap floating on the sea with the hand of a drowning man reaching up through the water toward it. This suggestion of the sinking of a ship and the attendant loss of life is undoubtedly more effective than an actual photograph depicting the tragedy in all its details. This same technique can be applied to the use of words. How can a dungeon be better described than by a reference to mouldy gray stones, the sound of dripping water, and the running feet of rats? Skillful reference to the rich tones of an organ and the dim shadows in the vaulted ceiling high overhead will create in the minds of the audience a better picture of the inside of a cathedral than a detailed description of choir and transept and nave. As one may form an impression of a man by the sound of his voice through a closed door or a glimpse of his shadow against a curtain, so may one gain a vivid impression from a mere suggestion couched in skillfully chosen language.

Where a lengthy description is advisable, the imaginative quality adds life and color to passages which might otherwise be dead and uninteresting. Depiction of people or objects in bare though accurate detail can prove tedious and lack power to command attention. Imaginative description awakes interest by reason of its dramatic quality as it

51

catches in a net of words the mood and the "feel" of an incident or a place and as it conveys the impression made by an individual rather than merely depicting physical appearance. By his choice of words, as well as by the construction of his phrases, the adroit preacher sets forth not only the facts which the conscious mind would register under given circumstances but also the psychological and emotional reaction which would be experienced. The description of a sunset and the coming of night should convey more than the fact that the sky was full of beautiful colors and that the sun dropped below the horizon and night came down. It should produce in the hearers something of the emotional feeling and mood which comes at the end of the day when they themselves see a sunset and are conscious of the creeping darkness as it settles around them.

In the use of suggestion and imagination the preacher employs metaphors and similes but uses them discreetly, being careful to keep his metaphors unmixed and his similes appropriate. Mr. Spurgeon furnished an excellent example as he spoke of the time "when this great universe lay in the mind of God like unborn forests in the acorn's cup."

To cultivate an ability to use these effective literary "tricks," a man needs to develop his own imaginative powers, to learn to observe and select important details, to become conscious not only of the actual objects he sees and of the words that he hears, but to become sensitive also of "atmosphere" and mood.

Ease and Spontaneity. A good sermon seems to flow from the heart of the preacher as a spring bubbles from the rocks. It has a quality of freshness about it. It is different from any other sermon because it has been copied from none. Ease and spontaneity, as the very words imply, mean a quality of unstudied smoothness. But the impression that ease and spontaneity in a sermon convey to the congregation is a false one. They are a technique of art most effective because most carefully concealed. Ease and spontaneity are the most difficult of all literary qualities to achieve. To do so there must be a great variety of expression and there must be an avoidance of overworked words and phrases. The ideas presented, though they may not be original with the speaker—and what speaker does have new ideas or fresh arguments—must be so acted upon by the chemistry of the preacher's mind as to come forth in a fresh form.

No preacher can give an impression of spontaneity who uses standard, hackneyed phrases, such as *each and every, sadder but wiser, feathered songsters, tired but happy, green with envy, take the bull by the horns, with bated breath, favor us with a selection, a goodly number*. No preacher can give an effect of ease who is trite and repetitious and monotonous.

Rhythm. A good sermon in common with good literature of other types possesses in its sentence structure as well as in its choice and arrangement of words a rhythmic quality which exerts a hypnotic effect upon the listener and when skillfully used encourages receptivity to the content of the sermon. It is largely this rhythmic quality, more obvious and highly developed, which lends charm to poetry and music. A preacher should not try to preach in blank verse; a sermon should not be written in iambic pentameter, but in all good pulpit prose there are definite, frequently changing rhythms. The preacher himself may not be aware of it, but unconsciously or deliberately the effective preacher uses the rhythmic beat in the construction of his sermon. It was Cicero who said, "The ear, or the mind through the ear, contains in itself a certain natural measure of all spoken sounds." As in a symphony there are frequent changes of tempo, so there will be changes in the rhythm of a sermon as the moods of the sermon change. An unchanging rhythm in construction, like an unchanging rhythm in delivery, will have one of two effects on an audience. It will, if rapid, make them very nervous. It will, if slow, induce somnolence.

It is to be most earnestly recommended that a preacher develop a good literary style. Reading great literature is a necessary step to this goal. There is no greater literature than the Word of God. The preacher should not only study the Bible for spiritual blessing and sermonic material; but he should also read it for its influence upon his own literary style. Shakespeare will develop the power of description, enlarge the vocabulary, fire the imagination of the man who reads and studies him. For polish and descriptive excellence no author excels Ruskin, and no preacher can afford to leave him unread.

VI

HOLDING THE
INTEREST OF AN AUDIENCE

IF A PREACHER intends to have anyone in his congregation except the faithful old saints who go to church Sunday after Sunday from a sense of duty and love for the Lord, it is imperative that he learn to gain the interest of his audience and preach in such a fashion as to hold that interest throughout his sermons. It is not enough that the preacher by force of personality attract interest in himself personally. If he is to accomplish anything by his ministry he must create interest also in his messages.

A carefully worded title is an excellent way to generate interest. The writers of books and the producers of plays and motion pictures are well aware of this fact. The preacher should be no less so. The subject and the title are not the same thing. The subject is the theme discussed; the title is the name given to the discussion. Occasionally the best title will be simply a statement of the subject, but as a rule the title should suggest the subject but not "give it away" altogether. The title should be in keeping with the type of the sermon and with the occasion for which the sermon has been built. A message intended for a great evangelistic campaign or mass meeting should have a different sort of title from one intended for a formal Sunday morning service. A spectacular and dramatic title which is suitable for the one would not be suitable for the other.

Good titles are generally concrete rather than abstract. A short title is better than a long one, and it should be as euphonious as possible. A paradoxical phrase may serve admirably as a title. Such a phrase arouses interest since it stimulates curiosity. Examples of this sort of title are "The Poor Rich Man," "An Honest Thief," "Full Yet Empty."

It is extremely important that the title be honest. An audience should feel that the title fits the message. For a congregation to go away with the feeling that the title has been deceptive is bad for the preacher. They lose confidence in his integrity and they become suspicious of the titles of future sermons when they hear them announced. There are some preachers who—particularly when engaged in Bible conference and evangelistic meetings—announce sensational titles which have no apparent relation to the sermons which they preach. In particular, advantage is taken of the appeal of prophecy to give titles having a prophetic suggestion to sermons which are not prophetic in character, and when prophetic messages are preached, the titles sometimes promise to reveal facts which the sermons do not disclose. Titles of this sort are unworthy of the ministry and unfair to the public. In this connection, it might be well to suggest that the title is not the only way in which the public is deceived in regard to prophetic messages. The announcements made from the pulpit at services preceding the one at which the message is to be preached are often couched in such terms as to promise definite facts when the message produces only vague generalities. Nothing has done more to discredit preaching on prophecy than sensationalism and dishonesty in the printed and pulpit announcements of prophetic sermons and in the title given to such messages.

A good subject for a sermon is easy to find. A good title is extremely difficult. Many conscientious preachers discover it is easier to build the sermon and preach it than to find a good title for it.

Having attracted the interest of an audience through the title, it is the preacher's obligation to himself and to his message to hold that interest. That preachers sometimes fail to do so springs from a failure to realize that there is a limit to human powers of concentration. We cannot expect to hold the concentrated interest of an audience indefinitely. The wise preacher will realize that his audience cannot because of physical and intellectual limitations remain interested in his message beyond a certain length of time. The period of time depends upon the audience. For an audience of young children a five- to seven-minute message is all that can be expected to do any good, and the speaker who can hold a child's interest as long as that is a good psychologist indeed. Certain types of adult audiences are little better. In preaching to a congregation made up of prisoners, for example, while there will likely be some highly intelligent men present, one deals for the most part with men of fairly low mentality, and from ten to fifteen minutes is long enough to attempt to hold their interest. Thirty minutes is as long as most preachers should expect to retain the interest of the average congregation. Many sermons which would have been good otherwise have been ruined by too great length, for there is such a thing as bringing a congregation beyond the point of decision. The listener may be convicted by the message and ready to make a decision and then lose interest or become irritated as the message is drawn out. It is a great gift to know when to quit. Luther said, "I would not have preachers torment their hearers and detain them with long and tedious preaching, for the delight of hearing vanishes therewith and the preachers hurt themselves."

The length of the sermon which a preacher may deliver without losing the interest of his hearers depends, too, upon the occasion and the circumstances. If, because of overlong preliminaries, the preacher does not get started until late, he will do well to shorten his message, since the audience will already be tired. If it is a morning service, the congregation will be conscious of the fact that it is getting near dinner time; if it is a night service, that it is being kept up rather late! It is unforgivable for a preacher to go overtime when he is on a program with other speakers or on a convention or Bible conference program which runs on a schedule. It is not fair to the other speakers on the program to take their time, and it shows decided conceit for a preacher to expect a congregation to prefer to listen to him instead of the other speaker upon whose time he is encroaching.

Psychologists tell us that the human mind is incapable of intensive concentration for any great length of time. The preacher should, therefore, provide rest periods during his message. With an average audience these should occur every five to seven minutes. These periods are particularly essential in a deep or technical message which demands hard thinking if the hearers are to follow the line of reasoning. If these points of relaxation are not provided, the mind of the hearer will relax without them and his thoughts will wander occasionally and the chain of the message will be broken. These rest points can be provided by a brief illustration, which Spurgeon compared to the engraving placed in the midst of the printed page of a book, or by a bit of narration, by a quotation of poetry, or simply by an interestingly worded sentence or two which does not demand an effort to understand and which, while in line with the thought, relieves the strain of continued concentration. These little rest periods cannot, of course, be arbitrarily inserted without relation to the message. They are not apart from the sermon; they are a part of it.

The preacher will find certain technical procedures useful in holding the attention of the audience throughout a message of reasonable length. Among the surest means of retaining interest is the use of variety—variety in vocal technique and variety in literary material. Any sort of monotony is deadly.

A preacher should practise frequent changes in speech rate, in pitch, and intensity. Any given rhythm of speech is effective only up to a certain point. If a speaker will observe his audience, he will note that after he has spoken for some time at a certain rate of speech a restlessness will develop. A complete break in rhythm and a change of tempo will remedy the condition and re-arrest attention which has begun to lag. An audience is not able to follow easily a line of thought presented for too long a time on the same pitch. However well a speaker may carry his audience along with him, he cannot expect to sustain a high pitch of dramatic or emotional intensity for too long. When he has reached a point of climactic intensity, he should relax and begin the next point on a lower level of intensity, even to the point of understressing. Here, then, is a good rule for the preacher: at the first sign of restlessness change the rate and the force and the pitch of speaking.

Good public speakers of every sort use great variety of material and all four literary types of discourse. There will be in the preacher's own material and in the quoted matter: exposition, argumentation, description, and narration. He will impart knowledge and make clear his own ideas. This is exposition. He will bring forth points to convince his hearers and he will present evidence. This is argumentation. He will draw word pictures of people, places, and things. This is description. He will recount the deeds of men. He will discuss history. He will tell what God has wrought. All this is narration.

While all four types of discourse will be used, they will not be used equally. Pure exposition which is addressed to the mind and leaves the emotions untouched becomes quickly tiresome. Argumentation which is based largely on conflict cannot be expected long to hold the interest of one who is not deeply concerned about the subject being argued or who does not hold deep conviction pro or con. Description, while it delights the ear and stimulates the imagination, is like a sweet—too much palls. Narration holds the attention in the long run better than the other forms since it does not detain the attention long at one point. Narration moves; it flows from event to event as it is fully developed, and narration sometimes includes in itself the other three forms of discourse. It is obvious that a sermon cannot be composed entirely of this type of discourse, but some narration should be included if the audience's attention is to be held. Anecdotes and incidents and stories used by way of illustration will introduce narration. Every sermon should include some description. In presenting his points, the preacher will enter the field of argumentation. Every good sermon obviously includes exposition.

Quoted material will lend variety. A verse of a hymn or a few lines of other poetry, quotations from the sermons of other men—all of these make for variety and, of course, the sermon will include quotations from the Scriptures.

It is not enough, however, to gain variety by the use of quoted material, but variety should be achieved in the introduction of such material. For example, one may introduce a poetic quotation by saying, "The poet has expressed the same idea in a different way," or "Gripped by the reality of this truth, someone has said," or "Isaac Watts weaves the idea into verse in this fashion." A Scriptural reference may be introduced thus: "The Holy Spirit gives us these words through John," "The Lord does not leave us ignorant on this point. Hear His words addressed to His disciples," "The Scriptures tell us," "Paul writing under divine inspiration said to the Corinthian church." Or the preacher may quote the Scripture without any introduction at all.

You will note that in none of the methods suggested have chapter and verse been given. Many preachers prefer to give the location of every verse quoted. Not only does the giving of chapter and verse each time make it difficult to achieve variety in introduction, but this practice also has other disadvantages. Some who have their Bibles will attempt to look up the references given and will lose the progression of the sermon and will be "left behind" while doing so. Others will try to remember the reference with the idea of looking it up when they get home and will miss the quotation as well as the next few moments of the message while trying to fix the reference in their minds. In teaching Bible classes, in lecturing to conference audiences where notebooks and pencils are the rule, references are perhaps advisable. In the ordinary sermon it can prove distracting. Of primary importance to the sermon and to the hearer is the Scripture itself—not chapter and verse.

Certain types of material and subject matter attract and hold attention. A reference to some incident which has recently occurred which is of local interest, a direct reference to some object or situation near at hand—in fact, any reference which strikes a chord of familiarity in the minds of the hearers—will attract the attention and rouse the interest of the listeners. The familiar, however, holds attention most strongly when it is used in connection with something which is unfamiliar or when something is said about the familiar which throws new light upon it or introduces some unusual fact about it. People are always interested in that which is of intimate and personal concern to them. A man will listen to that which he considers vital to himself. Therefore, to hold the attention of his hearers, the preacher should make the message strike home to the individual, make him feel that there is a matter of great personal concern in what the preacher is saying.

Another excellent procedure in holding the interest of the hearers is the dramatization of ideas. The speaker who can make the abstract seem concrete, the vague specific, will find the attention of the audience centered on his words. Dramatization is an especially successful method of dealing with figures and statistics. There is nothing especially arresting in the statement that it is 238,857 miles to the moon, but the preacher who says it would take an express train, traveling eighty miles an hour, approximately four months to reach the moon will not only give his hearers a better comprehension of the distance as he translates miles into months, but he will also interest them in the mere mention of great figures. The term "a billion dollars" does not mean much since the average man cannot conceive of a billion dollars. Reference to the national debt in figures of billions not only fails to convey any concrete impression to the hearers but the mention of such a gigantic figure sounds dull and a little frightening. But the preacher who describes a room "about twice as big as this auditorium" full of dollar bills can dramatize a figure which goes into billions in such a way that his hearers get some comprehension of the amount of the money and are interested. But not only figures and statistics can be dramatized. The preacher who says, "God opens the door of the day on golden hinges," is dramatizing an idea. Job dramatizes the same idea in a different way when he speaks of "the eyelids of the morning." *Pilgrim's Progress* is a dramatization of ideas from start to finish. Spurgeon dramatized his ideas regarding the use of notes by a preacher when he said, "Some go on crutches and read almost all their sermons. This, as a rule, must be a lame business. The most of us need to carry a staff, even if we do not often lean upon it." Another example of dramatization of ideas is this from Samuel Rutherford, "Christ's cross is the sweetest burden that ever I bore; it is such a burden as wings are to a bird, or sails to a ship, to carry me forward to my harbor." The man who can make ideas simple and concrete generally makes them gripping, and dramatization is the most effective method of making them simple and concrete. The effectiveness of good dramatization of ideas is illustrated by the incident recounted by Arthur H. Smith in his book *Preachers and Preaching*:

"Lord Chesterfield 'was listening in Lady Huntington's pew,' when Whitefield 'described the sinner under the character of a blind beggar led by a little dog. The dog escapes, from some cause, and he was left to grope his way guided only by his staff. Unconsciously he wanders to the edge of a precipice; his staff drops from his hand, down the abyss too far to send back an echo; he reaches forward cautiously to recover it; for a moment he poises on vacancy,' and then, while the whole congregation was tense with thrilled suspense, Chesterfield shouted, 'He is gone,' as he sprang from his seat to prevent the catastrophe. This was not simply the power of art and eloquence; alone, they are cold. But when they are set on fire by sincere warmth of feeling and conviction of truth, there is power to stir and move men to action. This, however, must be not a simulated earnestness. Reality alone stirs the heart of men."

The unexpected always attracts attention. A preacher can take advantage of this psychological principle to interest an audience. The speaker who says the unexpected or who says the usual in an unexpected fashion is an interesting speaker. Naturally a minister has to use this technique with great care. A conscientious preacher certainly will not shock his hearers by saying things unbecoming to a minister simply to attract attention, or by introducing subjects into the pulpit which have no place there, but it never lessens a man's power as a preacher if he occasionally surprises his congregation by saying or doing the unexpected. When a preacher's flock comes to expect the same type of sermon introduced by the same technique and based on the same type of outline Sunday after Sunday, the preacher has ceased to hold their attention and they do not look forward with much interest to hearing what he has to say. A man needs keen judgment and good hard common sense to know how far to go in the use of the unusual and unexpected, and legitimate use of this technique may easily degenerate into the cheap and sensational. Henry Ward Beecher was on dangerous ground when he auctioned off a colored slave girl from his Brooklyn pulpit; and the chances are that while he aroused interest and attracted attention, he did not accomplish unmitigated good.

Closely akin in principle to the surprise element is the technique of suspense. If a man knows how a story is going to turn out, he will not be as interested in the story as if he is held in suspense as to the outcome. A murder mystery holds the interest of its reader because he is held in suspense over "whodonit." The basis of successful storywriting as suggested by a magazine editor was: "Make 'em laugh. Make 'em cry. Make 'em wait."

If the preacher's style is such that the people always know exactly from the moment of beginning where he is going to come out, their interest will certainly lag. If a preacher can, rather early in his sermon, whet curiosity, keep it whetted, and hold off the moment of gratification until the close of the message he will have interested listeners. The use of suspense to hold attention can be especially well employed in narrative illustrations.

An interesting sermon will have points of climax. Audience interest will not be on the same level throughout. A good preacher should certainly "hold the attention of his audience from beginning to end," but that interest will have certain high points which the skillful preacher will carefully build up. There will be a climactic moment in each point which is developed and there will certainly be climax in the conclusion, and there should be one even in the introduction. As a general rule, up to the conclusion each climactic point will be higher than the one that has gone before. The highest point of climax will not always be in the conclusion. Possibly more often it will be in the very last point of the body of the sermon. Elsewhere we have referred to Spurgeon's theory of the sermonic climax—namely, that it "should end with the inculcation of some great, vital principle or some strong, majestic declaration of God—so that that principle or that declaration should be the highest peak of the range."

It is apparent then that the greatest secret of holding attention is change and movement. That which is static becomes commonplace and dull. A sermon should progress. It should go somewhere, but it should move like a circus parade, not like a wedding procession. It will be made up of a great variety of elements. As in a circus parade there are elephants, animals in cages, calliopes, bands, and clowns, so the sermon will be made up of a wide variety of materials. The clowns are scattered along the procession like the rest periods which should be provided in the sermon. We are surprised to see a dog riding a pony and a waltzing horse. We are held in suspense by the juggler who seems always on the verge of dropping the plates. Our curiosity is whetted by the closed wagons, heavily gilded and carved, and we wonder what is inside. The idea of romance is dramatized by the fairy-tale prince and princess. The most interesting things in the parade are not crowded all together, but scattered out. A circus parade has points of climax. So should a sermon.

VII

PSYCHOLOGICAL BASES OF APPEAL

A SERMON SHOULD BE SOUND from the standpoint of thought. It should show clear thinking on the part of the preacher and a knowledge of his subject. His points should be clearly set forth and accurately presented.

The sermon should be addressed to the intelligence level of the average man or woman, and the preacher should bear in mind that the average man or woman is not a profound thinker, and cannot be expected to follow long and involved reasoning. The sermon should be so planned that a man of average intelligence, as he follows the line of thought from point to point, will consciously or unconsciously conclude, "That sounds reasonable," "That seems true," "That is convincing." In other words, the preacher should set forth the claims of Christ in such a reasonable and logical fashion that his hearers are convinced of the justice of the claims.

A preacher should be logical in his treatment of the text and the development of his arguments. The interpretation of the text should be in accord with the context. There should be a logical progression from point to point in the outline. There must be no loose and inconclusive reasoning. When you set out to prove a point, you should prove it. If an idea is important, develop it. If it is not important enough to be worth developing, it had better be omitted, since to include it distracts the attention of the hearers from the more important points.

Comparisons should be completed logically (and it might be well to add in this connection that the mixed metaphor is the result of illogical thinking). Statements should not contradict or seem to contradict each other, nor should there be any contradiction in the connotation of the words which are used. It is poor logic to say, *"Faithful* Peter denied his Lord thrice."

The conclusions reached should be warranted by the evidence. When a sermon undertakes to set forth evidence of a fact it should present every part of the evidence which an intelligent listener has a right to expect, and the conclusion arrived at must be warranted by the evidence presented. Logical reasoning does not run in a circle, that is, it does not make an assumption to prove a statement and then use the statement to prove the assumption. One must not, for example, say: "Prohibition is evil because it produces lawlessness. How do I know there is lawlessness? Because lawlessness always accompanies prohibition."

The logical preacher will not generalize from an insufficient number of incidents or on insufficient evidence. He will realize that whatever is illogical in the construction and development of his sermon hurts the cause of the Gospel.

The Word of God is logical. God's plan of salvation is a logical plan. God's invitation is, "come now and let us reason together," but the appeal of the Gospel is more than an appeal to human reasoning, and it is not enough that a sermon be coldly logical and addressed to the intellect. Such a sermon is bound to be purely technical and academic and will not move an audience to action. That which appeals to the head alone cannot produce results in the life. That which moves to action must appeal to certain inherent human emotions, desires, and instincts. A preacher must touch these if he expects to stimulate his hearers to something more than mere intellectual acquiescence. These basic motives may be said to be not of the head but of the heart, since they have their roots not in logic but in an impulsive inward urge, inherent and instinctive.

The value of an appeal to the emotions is recognized by successful writers as well as by great orators and preachers. Some modern ministers profess to address themselves almost entirely to the intellectual in their preaching, confusing the motive appeal with emotionalism. (Actually, it is to be doubted that a preacher can avoid some appeal to the primary motives in his sermon, as they are so definitely a part of life, so closely interwoven into the complexity of our being that our very thought processes are motivated by them.)

There has been an overemphasis on cold, academic discussion, even in orthodox pulpits. This tendency has developed largely as a result of cowardly regard for the criticism of the enemies of the Gospel who maintain that any demonstration of feeling in spiritual affairs is a sign of mental or emotional instability and weakness. It is interesting that such criticism is not advanced against a show of emotional reaction in any other phase of life, but is confined entirely to the realm of religious experience. A man who becomes excited over baseball, who screams himself hoarse and throws pop bottles at the umpire, is called a fan, but when he shows any signs of emotion or excitement in connection with his religious experience he is called a fanatic. It is to be granted there can be an unwholesome emotionalism in religion, an uncontrolled display of which sometimes

66

takes the place of a genuine heartfelt experience of conviction and conversion. It is even to be granted that an abnormal emotionalism is encouraged by certain sects. The wholesome, normal course lies between this extreme and the opposite extreme of deadness and spiritual unconcern, and the one can be about as bad as the other. A man's mind is informed; nothing more is accomplished. A man's impulses are stirred; action results. Therefore, the motive appeal is important in preaching, since a preacher's business is not chiefly to change men's minds but to change their lives. To these motive appeals Satan makes his advances. A man sins because he is moved to sin through one of these avenues of motive appeal. The movies, the theater, the novelist use them. To them advertising addresses itself. These basic desires are infinite in number. Some of them are closely related. Many of them overlap. Unharnessed, uncontrolled, and unconsecrated, they may lead a life to destruction, but controlled and harnessed they build institutions and civilizations. Consecrated and dedicated to God, they inspire to service and enrich the world. Some of them the preacher will not often use; some he will possibly never use. Some will be embodied in the illustrations which he uses to stimulate interest but will not be touched upon in the message itself. Some of the basic emotions to which the preacher can appeal are love of friends, love of family, loyalty, patriotism, desire for companionship, the appeal of adventure, self-respect, self-preservation, fear, sympathy, generosity, curiosity, desire for immortality.

The use of arguments or illustrations appealing to any of his finer instincts cannot be reasonably objected to, provided the effort is sincerely and appropriately made and provided that this technique is not overworked. Skillful professional lecturers and politicians know, as do many effective preachers, that a sure way to gain interest and stir their listeners to a mood of response is to dwell upon such themes as love of mother, love of native land, and similar topics. A story inserted by way of an illustration dealing with the love and faithfulness of a mother has been known to touch the heart of a sinner as it brings to mind his own godly mother. God has many times used such a story to soften the hearts of men hardened from years of sin, and many of them have found Christ. The sincere preacher will differentiate between sentiment and sentimentality in the use of such illustrations. The one is genuine and lofty; the other cheap and insincere.

But not only are there these lofty emotions to which a sermon may appeal. There are others which may be stirred. For example, the emotion of vicarious fear is freely played upon in the development of many short stories, plays, and murder mysteries. Why should not the preacher use an appeal to this emotion, not as a vicarious thing but personally and genuinely? The fear of hell may not be the best reason for a sinner's turning to Christ, but any reason which brings a man to the foot of the cross is a good reason. Psychologists and the liberal preachers have joined in deriding the preaching of Jonathan Edwards, with its emphasis on hell and judgment, but Edwards' sermon on the "Sinner in the Hands of an Angry God" produced results. The hearts of his hearers were touched, they were convicted of their sins, and they cried out for mercy and forgiveness under the spell of a sermon so powerful that they seemed to feel themselves actually falling into hell. Every preacher could not deal with hell and the judgment so skillfully and effectively as Jonathan Edwards, but no preacher should avoid an appeal to any emotion of the human heart, be it love or fear, which produces results as God blesses it to the salvation of souls. Fear of sin and its blight and disgrace is a wholesome emotion and one that needs to be cultivated in this day when sin is so lightly regarded. Until a man knows a sense of the awfulness of sin, until he feels convinced of his own sinfulness, he does not feel the need of the cleansing blood of Christ.

There is in every individual a more or less highly developed sense of curiosity. It is this that gives impetus to study and research, that makes the archeologist dig up buried civilization, the scientist wear himself out in the laboratory. Of a less lofty quality it impels a woman, or even a man, to pry into a neighbor's private affairs. The proficient preacher takes advantage of this human quality, by first arousing curiosity, then whetting it, and finally satisfying it.

Often the preacher may appeal to more than one of these inherent qualities in the same sermon. Sometimes he may approach his congregation from more than one basis at once. For example, a "human interest" story may appeal to both curiosity and sympathy. The story may excite curiosity to awaken interest and then touch a chord of emotional response in the hearts of the listeners.

Emotions are of the heart. The heart of the sinner must be softened by the Gospel and changed by saving grace. The heart of the saint must be warmed. One of the great needs of the average Christian is "a heart resigned, submissive, meek." The preacher should have these heart-needs of his congregation in mind while preaching. A sermon that does not touch the heart will not deeply touch the life. After hearing Massillon, the Bishop of Clermount, preach, King Louis XIV of France said to him, "Father, I have heard many great orators in this chapel; I have been highly pleased with them: but for you, whenever I hear you, I go away displeased with myself; for I see more of my own character." If a man goes out of church feeling pleased with himself, the sermon has been a failure. The hymn writer has said, "May the Gospel's joyful sound conquer sinners, comfort saint," but the comfort which the hearing of the Gospel brings to God's child is not the comfort of self-satisfaction but the comfort of a new realization of the forgiveness and grace and love of God bestowed upon him in Christ Jesus.

A sermon should be instructive in the truth of God, but it should offer more than instruction. There should be inspiration, stimulation, and conviction. The preacher achieves these by an emotional appeal and not by an intellectual one. In conclusion, let it be noted again that there should not be overemphasis on emotionalism, but the emotions should be stirred. The mind may be convinced, but the heart must be converted. The preacher who permits the lecturer and politician to show himself more skillful in handling techniques of audience motivation, wiser in his use of the various avenues of approach to his hearers, would seem to admit thereby that entertainment and instruction and politics are more important than the Gospel.

VIII

THE DELIVERY OF THE SERMON

IT IS INTERESTING to note that the majority of books dealing with the subject of homiletics have a great deal to say about the preparation of sermons and comparatively little about the delivery of them. For example, John Broadus in his book, *A Treatise on the Preparation and Delivery of Sermons,* out of a total of twenty chapters devotes only three to the subject of delivery, the longest of these being a treatise upon the three methods of sermon delivery, not a discussion of technique of delivery so much as a historical investigation into the three methods—reading, recitation, and extemporaneous speaking from the pulpit. Perhaps this practice of allotting relatively little space to the delivery of sermons in books on homiletics is due to the fact that much of the material in all textbooks or reference works in the field of speech apply, at least so far as the general principles are concerned, to pulpit speech as well as to that of any other type of public discourse. On the other hand, though any good work dealing with the development of a smooth literary style may be studied with considerable profit

70

oy the minister who wishes to improve the literary quality of his sermon, on the actual matter of sermon construction no books are available except those dealing exclusively with homiletics.

In the present volume much has already been said upon the matter of the actual delivery of sermons, both in the chapter, "Holding the Interest of an Audience," and also the chapter, "The Preacher and His Voice." There are some further pertinent suggestions which should be made.

Whether a sermon be read from a manuscript, delivered from memory, or preached more or less extemporaneously from a prepared outline, it is intended to be delivered orally to an audience. Though it be conceived in the mind of the preacher and developed through hours of preparation and study, it does not become *alive* until it is preached. However perfectly formed the sermon may be, if it is not well delivered it suffers greatly in consequence. It is a dead thing—"still born." All those great preachers who have attained to any sort of ministerial immortality—if we may be permitted such a phrase—those who have achieved a lasting reputation—have been men who were effective and powerful in the pulpit. Most of them were also masters of the art of sermonic construction but by no means all of them, for in reading the sermons left behind in manuscript by some of these men one is convinced that their greatness of reputation rests evidently on some other basis than on the quality of their sermons. We are almost forced to the conclusion that a poor sermon well delivered is preferable to a good sermon poorly preached.

In addition to the benefit to the preacher of a voice well developed and trained to flexibility and variety, and in addition to the knowledge of the techniques of holding the interest and attention of an audience, there are certain other technical points which contribute to effectiveness of sermonic delivery.

An effective preacher must know how to secure proper emphasis and where to place it. Some men seek to dominate an audience by sheer force and volume. They attempt to emphasize the entire sermon and have, therefore, no powers in reserve to use at climactic and important points. The secret of emphasis lies in the matter of contrast. A clearing in a forest is as noticeable as a single tree rising in the midst of an empty plain. In both cases it is the contrast which arrests the attention. So in preaching, that which the preacher would have the hearers particularly notice must by his delivery contrast with the material surrounding it.

In almost every sentence there are certain words which should stand out. In every paragraph there are certain sentences which are more important than others, and in the sermon there are certain paragraphs which deserve particular attention. How then can we by contrast focus these sharply upon the ear, and so upon the mind of the hearers? There are only four ways in which this emphasis in speaking can be effected. Upon the use of one or a combination of more than one of these simple speech techniques the speaker must rely if he is to avoid a common level of monotony in his speech. Emphasis must depend upon, first, a change in pitch, or a variation in range; second, a change in force, stress, or volume; third, a change in the rate or tempo of speech; and fourth, the use of pauses. Let us, however, for the sake of simplicity, and that by means of alliteration we may fix them in our minds, call these four speech techniques simply: pitch, punch, progress, and pause.

Let us see how emphasis may be achieved through the uses of each of these four techniques.

Pitch. In a sentence spoken almost entirely on a dead level of pitch one word spoken a tone or two higher than the rest will stand out. A word spoken on a downward, sliding inflection will stand out in marked contrast to words spoken on an even pitch. In the same way a whole sentence spoken a bit higher or a bit lower in range than the rest of the paragraph will stand out.

Punch. This is the commonest method of securing emphasis and it is one upon which many preachers rely almost entirely, particularly those who have not developed resonance and flexibility of voice and who have not learned the value of vocal variety and changing tempos in speech. This form of emphasis consists simply in putting more power behind the voice in speaking certain words or phrases. It depends upon the use of greater volume or a more explosive type of delivery at emphatic points.

Progress. Emphasis as well as variety can be obtained by the change of the rhythm of one's speech. Here again the secret of the whole matter is found in contrast. A brief sentence or two spoken more slowly than the rest of the speech will be emphatic because it is in such startling contrast with the other material. Emphasis is more generally achieved by retarding the portion to be accentuated rather than by speeding up that portion, since the audience is much more apt to hear that which is spoken slowly than that which is spoken with great rapidity.

Pause. A word or phrase spoken just after a pause will stand out from that which has gone before. For special stress a pause may be used immediately after the word or phrase as well as before it, thus lending double emphasis.

A good preacher in the course of a sermon will make considerable use of all four forms of emphasis and will more often use two or more in combination than any single form by itself. The less a preacher depends upon one method of securing interest and the more he cultivates the use of all four methods, the more effective will be his pulpit delivery.

PROJECTION

One cannot overemphasize the fact that good public speaking is not different from good conversational speech. It is simply an enlargement of conversational speech. An effective preacher avoids unnaturalness of speech in the pulpit. His voice and his style are his own, the same which he uses in conversation with friends or family, but enlarged to reach across the greater distance which separates the pulpit from the pew, and projected to fill the auditorium.

For effectiveness in delivery nothing takes the place of deep sincerity and strong conviction. The preacher who preaches with conviction speaks from his heart and there is power in such preaching. If he believes earnestly in the truth of what he is saying and is convinced that it has great importance for his hearers and that they should be persuaded by the truth which he is speaking, a man will speak with fervor and power. All the technical knowledge and training in the art of speech which a man can acquire will not take the place of this sense of conviction and responsibility.

It is this pouring out of himself which makes the preaching of a sermon a difficult task. A man so inspired from within himself will not make an effort to "save" himself and conserve his energy while he preaches. He will give abundantly of himself and when he finishes his message will find himself at a point of nervous tension and exhilaration, but an hour afterwards will begin to feel the exhaustion which comes from the spiritual, mental, and physical effort of preaching. This is the thing which Gregory of Nazianzen must have in mind when he spoke of the "tempest of spirit" which a minister experiences. It is the sense of responsibility which goes with such deep conviction which must have led St. Cyran to say, "I would rather say a hundred masses than preach one sermon."

Effective delivery depends upon a strong will concentrated upon the task of dominating and holding one's hearers. A dynamic speaker is somewhat of an expert in mass hypnosis. He faces his audience with the conscious determination that they shall listen to him, get what he has to say to them, and respond as he *wills* that they shall respond. Never during the entire course of the sermon does the preacher relax

74

this intent concentration of will power. Speech teachers sometimes say to their pupils, "When you speak in public talk to the man on the last row. If he hears you, so will everyone else." That is good advice, but the man who *wills* that each individual in his congregation shall hear him and respond to his message will more effectively accomplish his purpose than the preacher who simply speaks to the man on the last row. An audience, however respectable and cultivated and civilized it may be, is not simply a composite of the individuals who make it up. That is, emotionally and intellectually it is not such a composite. Something of the personality of an individual is submerged when he becomes one of a crowd. Therefore, though an effective preacher addresses each individual and makes him feel he is being preached to personally, the effective preacher must also *dominate* the crowd as a whole.

A preacher will find that by an effective use of his eyes, by a direct glance into the face of his hearers he can do much to hold their attention and dominate their thinking. It is, therefore, greatly to be desired that there be a strong light upon the face of the preacher at such an angle that his eyes are not thrown into shadow. A good dramatic producer would not think of having a character on the stage with his face in the shadow for an important scene, but Sunday after Sunday preachers in gloomy churches propound the eternal truths of God to congregations who have only the dimmest view of their faces. It is not important that the preacher see his audiences clearly, but it is of utmost importance that the audience have a clear view of the preacher. They are thus enabled to see not only his eyes but the full play of emotion across his countenance.

Bourdaloue, who was well known for his oratory, it is said, kept his eyes half-closed while preaching in order that he might not find his thoughts diverted from the carefully prepared material of his message. He would have been more effective had he learned the value of the preacher's eye as it gazes upon the countenance of the hearers, but probably

75

the churches in which he preached were so gloomy that even had he had his eyes tightly closed the audience would not have known the difference. There is many a preacher in America whose pulpit is so poorly lighted that his congregation would not be aware of it if he preached with his eyes closed.

GESTURES

Another phase of pulpit speech which should receive some consideration is the matter of gestures. They are a physical means of conveying ideas or impressions or of lending emphasis to those verbally expressed. A man should never use a gesture unless he feels an urge to do so, since the only effective gesture is a natural gesture. It should be the spontaneous expression of inner feeling. To imitate deliberately another man's gestures is to develop an artificial and unnatural mode of expression. There is a story that one of Billy Sunday's many imitators not only prepared a manuscript of one of his messages but also made notes of the gestures and actions with which Mr. Sunday accompanied his words. Once as he was preaching this sermon he overlooked one of the notations, only to remember it some sentences later. He stopped to apologize to his audience and said, "I forgot something." He went back and repeated the paragraph, this time including the gesture. Whether there is any truth in the story or not, it shows what a fool imitation can make of a man.

The preacher should seek to cultivate grace and ease of gesture. He should try to overcome awkwardness and learn to use his body in a graceful fashion. His gestures should be graceful and easy because he has developed habits of grace and ease, because grace and ease are natural to him, not because he attempts to make a graceful gesture.

No better advice has ever been given in regard to gestures than that included in Shakespeare's advice to the players in *Hamlet,* "Suit the action to the word, the word to the action." Gestures should be a natural part of the expression of thought, but are most effective when not too frequent.

Ask someone to describe an accordion or a spiral stair and see how automatically he uses his hands in giving the description. Such gestures are spontaneous. So should the preacher's be in the pulpit. If you feel the need of a gesture in making a point emphatic use a gesture, but avoid constant repetition of the same gesture or a whirling of the arms like windmills.

Here are some suggestions about what not to do in gesturing. Do not shake your finger in the face of the audience. There may be a time when a finger pointed at the hearers will be extremely effective. Shaking your finger at them never is. It is only irritating. Avoid puny, finical gestures and tight, stiff gestures too close to the body. They convey an impression of pettiness, petulance, and weakness. Such gestures generally spring from self-consciousness and are an indication of some complex or inhibition from which the preacher should seek to free himself.

IX

THE PREACHER AND HIS VOICE

OF WHITEFIELD it was said:

"With a full and beaming countenance, and the frank and easy port which the English people love, he combined a voice of rich compass, which could equally thrill over Moorfields in musical thunder or whisper its terrible secret in every private ear; and to his gainly aspect and tuneful voice he added a most expressive and eloquent action." *

* Arthur H. Smith, *Preachers and Preaching* (Philadelphia: The United Lutheran Publication House, 1925), p. 107.

The preacher's chief tool of his trade is his voice, yet the development of the instrument itself and of skill in its use is shamefully neglected in training for the ministry. It is just as important to know how to deliver a sermon successfully as it is to know how to build one successfully. No athlete would consider himself trained for competitive sport who had simply become acquainted with the rules of the game. The athlete considers the development of his body equally important. He not only tries to learn the game, but he also tries by exercise and diet to build a body strong and supple enough to enable him to participate skillfully and successfully. So, in the case of the preacher, it is not enough to know the rules of sermon making. There should be a development of the instrument of delivery and, through exercise and practice, of skill in its use.

Every public speaker needs to know something of the physical construction of the vocal mechanism if he is successfully to develop and use it. A technical physiological discussion would be out of place here, but a brief and general analysis of the component part of the voice-producing mechanism will be profitable.

The vocal mechanism may be conveniently considered in four parts.

The Chest Portion. In the upper cavity of the body are (1) the lungs, which serve as the air chambers; (2) the bronchial tubes, which connect the lungs with the windpipe, forming an outlet for the release of the air; (3) the bones and the binding cartilages and tissues to which the lungs are fastened and which afford leverage for the application of power; and (4) the muscles which pump the air into and out of the lungs. This pumping is accomplished not only by the muscles in the chest itself but also by the abdominal muscles lying beneath the lungs and by the diaphragm. Thus, there is not only a pressure outward but also a pressure downward in exhaling and a pressure not only outward but also upward in inhaling.

The Larynx. The larynx, composed of a group of small

cartilages intertwined with muscles, is situated at the upper end of the windpipe. The vocal bands, commonly called vocal cords, are contained in the larynx. Speech tone is produced by vibration caused by the air exhaled from the lungs as it passes between and against the vocal bands which have been drawn together by muscular action. Change in pitch is effected by the tension of the cords and the amount of space between them.

The Amplifiers. The upper part of the larynx itself, the throat, the head cavities, including the sinuses and the mouth, act as resonating chambers to amplify the sound which originates in the larynx. Their purpose is somewhat the same as that accomplished by the hollow portion or sound board of a stringed musical instrument, which serves to increase the volume of the sound made by the strings. These resonating cavities also serve to modify the quality of the tone and in some of them the vowel sounds are formed.

The Modifiers. The shape of the resonating chambers is changed by the movement of the palate, jaws, teeth, lips, tongue, and back wall of the pharynx, and the quality of the tone is thereby affected. Consonant sounds are formed by them as they interrupt the steady flow of the mere vocal tone. Without them there would be no *l, p, t, d, s, r,* and related sounds.

From this very brief and very nontechnical glimpse into the physical mechanism of speech production, it is apparent that effective speaking must depend primarily upon a healthy mechanism, well-controlled. Any preacher, unless suffering from some physical malformation or unless he has greatly abused his voice by incorrect use over a long period of years, can develop the physical possibilities of his vocal instrument and learn proper control of it.

First of all, it is advisable that the lung capacity be developed and essential that breathing be properly controlled. A large chest capacity is desirable, although it is not so important to the preacher as to the singer, since the one chiefly uses short tones and the other sustained tones. Breath control is tremendously important because the volume of air leaving the lungs and the force with which it is expelled primarily govern the power of the tone. The exercises recommended by physical instructors for the development of chest expansion will increase the capacity of the lungs. For developing breath control a good exercise is to fill the lungs with air and exhale *very slowly,* as nearly as possible emptying the lungs. The same procedure may be followed by expelling the air on a hummed tone or on the various vowel sounds, using one complete breath for each vowel. A good way to test one's breath control is to place a lighted candle a few inches in front of the mouth and exhale completely. With proper breath control, there will be only the slightest flicker of the flame.

There is not much which can be done for the development of the larynx itself, but one can, however, cultivate a relaxed throat. The best thing one can do for his throat is to keep himself in good general physical condition. When one is tired or sick it shows in the voice. The muscles which control the larynx lose their tonicity when there is a general physical debilitation. A speaker should seek to overcome tension of the throat, since this produces soreness and leads to strain which will eventually damage the vocal apparatus. During the latter part of the nineteenth century, hoarseness, roughness of voice, and a tired condition of the larynx were referred to as "clergyman's throat." The term was not complimentary to the speech technique of the pulpit since such a throat condition was regarded as more or less to be expected in preachers and the natural result of the use of the voice in preaching. When he is well physically, the preacher should not experience sore throat as a result of preaching, and he will not experience it if he uses his speech mechanism properly. As this type of sore throat develops primarily from tension in the muscles of the neck and throat, a good way to avoid it is to prepare one's sermon well, as a sense of confidence in one's preparation makes for relaxation. One can develop a relaxed condition of the throat by avoiding nervous tension and cultivating a relaxed physical condition generally. Exercises which relax the neck are excellent. Often, yawning and then singing the vowel sounds will relax the throat. The *habit* of relaxation can be developed.

A preacher should remember that immediately after preaching, his entire body is likely to be damp with perspiration and his vocal mechanism to be "warmed up." To avoid taking cold, he should be careful not to become too quickly chilled, and he should by all means beware of drafts. Particularly, however, should he beware of going immediately out of doors in cold weather, even if warmly wrapped, since breathing cold air into a larynx "warm" from speaking can produce huskiness and a serious throat inflammation. Drinking ice water immediately after speaking is also unwise. A man who has just preached strenuously will be thirsty, especially in hot weather, but moderately cool water will quench his thirst without the sudden shock which ice water will give his throat.

There is nothing much that can be done to develop the tongue and the jaws and the lips after maturity. During childhood and adolescence much can be done through proper diet, but once maturity is reached, the physical construction has taken its final shape. Though he cannot *develop* them, the preacher should learn to *use* his jaws and his tongue and his lips. All three are intended to move in the production of words. The English language cannot be properly spoken with a tight lower jaw. The preacher should cultivate a loose jaw, supple lips, and an active tongue. If the jaws are kept too close together, all sounds will be muffled. If the tongue does not move properly, all sounds will be "mushy." If the lips do not move, all sounds will be mumbled, particularly consonant sounds.

Good exercise for the development of facility of the lips, tongue, and jaws are the tongue-twisters: "Susan sells seashells on the seashore"; "Three, three, three slim, slim sleek saplings"; "Peter Piper picked a peck of pickle peppers," etc. To read aloud rapidly the words of some of the "patter-songs" of Gilbert and Sullivan is also good exercise for the instruments of articulation.

So much then for the development of the vocal organs and the acquisition of facility in their use. A great voice is a wonderful gift, and all the exercise and training in the world will not give a man a great voice if he has not the natural physical possibilities. Every preacher cannot be as "golden-mouthed" as Chrysostom, nor as richly voiced as Whitefield, who, it is said, spoke the word "Mesopotamia" in a tone to make strong men weep. But one can make the most of the voice which God has given him.

The first essential of good public speaking is that the speaker be heard. If a man has something worth saying, it is worth hearing; and if a speaker cannot be heard, there is no point in his speaking. It is important that every person in the building get the message and, therefore, *to be heard should be the first concern of the preacher when he begins to speak.* The same application of speech technique which will guarantee that an audience of a hundred in a small room will hear the message will not be satisfactory in a building which seats several thousand.

Today one usually finds a public address system in large buildings. However, a man who speaks in various auditoriums is going to find himself, some time or other, in a large building—or in a smaller building with poor acoustics, which is infinitely worse than a large building with good acoustics —with no microphone in front of him and no amplifier to "boost" his voice. The use of the public address system is, by the way, a concession to the lack of training on the part of our speakers and the auditory laziness of a modern audience. The great speakers of other days were clearly understood by the occupants of the last pew in great barn-like buildings that seated thousands. Today even the most proficient and self-confident speaker would develop a case of acute stage fright at the thought.

In other generations preachers made themselves audible to multitudes totaling many thousands without the aid of any sort of amplification except that which was afforded by the topography of the countryside or the surrounding buildings of the city. George Whitefield was such a speaker. Benjamin Franklin said of him:

"He had a loud and clear voice, and articulated his words and sentences so perfectly, that he might be heard and understood at a great distance, especially as his auditories, however numerous, observed the most exact silence. He preached one evening [in Philadelphia] from the top of the Court-House steps, which are in the middle of Market Street, and on the west side of Second Street, which crosses it at right angles. Both streets were filled with his hearers to a considerable distance. Being among the hindmost in Market Street, I had the curiosity to learn how far he could be heard, by retiring backwards down the street towards the river; and I found his voice distinct till I came near Front Street, when some noise in that street obscured it. Imagining then a semicircle, of which my distance should be the radius, and that it were filled with auditors, to each of whom I allowed two square feet, I computed that he might well be heard by more than thirty thousand. This reconciled me to the newspaper accounts of his having preached to twenty-five thousand people in the fields, and to the ancient histories of generals haranguing whole armies, of which I had sometimes doubted." *

It is well for a preacher to remember that the average man today has a sense of hearing which has been so coddled by science and engineering that it has ceased to exert itself. This is a generation used to loud voices on the radio, to amplified voices in movie houses, theaters, and lecture halls. We have lost the habit of listening intently. We have not had to make an effort to hear because the turn of a

* D. H. Montgomery, *Benjamin Franklin; His Life* (Boston: Ginn & Company, 1906), p. 139.

knob has increased the volume of sound so that we have been able to hear without listening. The preacher who expects his congregation to make an effort to hear him is a deluded man. It is up to the preacher to make himself heard.

To be heard depends primarily upon two things. It depends first upon sufficient volume to carry the sound. The power of the voice must be great enough to carry the vocal sounds to every part of the building. The speaker should beware, however, of raising pitch as he increases volume. Too often "raising your voice" means raising the pitch as well as increasing the power. It is difficult to speak louder without speaking on a higher tone. Practice and concentration are both required to overcome this tendency.

It is always important that the voice should be properly "placed," but at no time more so than when speaking at full volume. Improper placement will not only injure the throat but will also make for an unpleasant tone and cause rapid tiring of the throat. Here is a good exercise for proper placement of tone. With the lips closed hum a tone so that vibration will be felt in the front part of the face. Then go directly on the same tone into an enunciation of "me, me, me, me," being careful to maintain the same placement tone. This exercise will enable you to discover the proper placement of your voice and to acquire the habit of such placement.

Many speakers whose volume is for the most part sufficient to enable them to be satisfactorily heard, have a habit of dropping the voice at the end of sentences, phrases, and paragraphs. Many times if the last word or so of a sentence is missed the meaning of the sentence is missed. The audience thinks it has not heard it at all because it has not heard enough to get the idea the speaker has been trying to express. The listeners may just as well not hear any of the speaker's words as to miss so large a portion as to lose the meaning of what he is saying.

Volume alone is not enough to make one heard. Good

enunciation is essential. Vowel and consonant sounds must be fully formed. Consonant sounds must not be dropped, and vowel sounds must be given their proper value. Words must be finished. It is just as important that the last syllable of a word be fully formed as it is that the volume of tone be kept up to the end of the sentence. Some speakers with powerful voices which carry well cannot be understood because the resonant quality of the voice, with its heavy low tones, blurs the words spoken. One tone carries over into another. With voices of this type special effort must be made to secure good enunciation. With this type of voice less volume may make the audience hear better than greater, since the overtones will not be then so prominent. The effect of too much volume with this type of voice is similar to that of a radio turned on too loud. The voice of the speaker can be heard a block away but one close by finds it difficult to understand the words.

It is not enough, however, for a speaker to be heard and his words understood simply as words. The speaker's ideas should be heard as ideas. That is to say, the audience should get the meaning of the message. Let us take for granted that the speaker has some ideas to put over and that they are well organized. The emphasis which he gives to his words will convey them to the audience. The same sentence can mean many things. An ordinary proper name of one syllable—Jack, or Bill, or Jim—can be spoken in such a fashion as to convey any one of a number of different meanings: a request for help, a plea to be heard, a term of reproach, etc. The impression upon the hearer will depend upon the inflection or emphasis. In a similar fashion a sentence can mean any number of different things, depending upon the way the sentence is spoken. A simple sentence oftentimes has as many meanings as there are words in the sentence. The meaning can be altered by altering the emphasis.

It is possible by subtlety of emphasis to say more than the words themselves actually mean. Indeed, it is possible to convey an opposite meaning to that which the words themselves actually express. An example of the latter is seen in the use of sarcasm—something, by the way, for which a preacher should find very little use.

There is more to conveying an idea than emphasis and inflection. Quality and tempo assist. The quality of the voice should vary to suit the subject and the occasion. A serious quality of voice is suited to a serious narrative, lighter quality of voice to a more casual narrative, dramatic intensity to a narrative of suspense or excitement. The quality of the voice should change in the course of a sermon and the voice should be colored in quality to suit the changing moods of the message.

The rate of speaking should also be varied. Most speakers average from 120 to 150 words a minute. This rate is not arrived at by machine-like regularity of utterance. The tempo should vary with the ideas expressed. A humorous story would not demand the same slow and deliberate speed which should be used for a weighty or solemn matter. In building to a climax one should increase his tempo. Note how the same announcer will use an entirely different quality and much more rapid tempo in broadcasting a play-by-play account of a sport's event from that which he uses in introducing the speaker on a religious broadcast.

The preacher should make the Gospel attractive to men. It is not enough to give them the Gospel, but it should be presented in such a way as to make men accept it. To this end the preacher should seek for a pleasant quality of voice. Unpleasant quality of tone, nasality, harshness, a whine or twang can mar the beauty of the voice. There is no musical instrument more beautiful than a well-trained, well-placed voice, and while the preacher's first concern in preaching should not be the sound of his own voice, he owes it to the message which he is called to give men to seek through practice to acquire a pleasant voice. The way some preachers use their voices can be compared with an organist at the console of a great organ who confines himself to playing on one note and using only one stop. The average human voice is capable of development to a range of at least two octaves. The preacher should find what is for him the normal tone of speaking, but he should not confine himself to that one tone. He should use the notes above and below it, not only for beauty but also for variety of speech.

A lack of change in rhythm, mood, and pitch, makes for a "speech pattern" than which there is nothing more tiresome to an audience. The ministerial tone, "the holy whine," will be avoided by sufficient variety in the use of pitch, rhythm, and mood.

One of the great difficulties in overcoming bad voice quality and habits of speech is our inability to hear our own voices. Our speech does not sound to us as it sounds to other people. Every preacher should, therefore, have a recording made. He will then be able to hear approximately how his voice sounds to others. If possible a recording should be made of an actual sermon as it is preached from the pulpit, and for best results and to avoid self-consciousness it would be better if such a record could be made without the preacher's knowledge. At any rate, such a record should be made during the preaching of a sermon. Most radio stations are equipped to make recordings, and for a nominal cost they will be glad to record a sermon which they are broadcasting. A preacher whose Sunday morning services are "put on the air" would do well to have at least one such recording made. The chances are that as for the first time he hears his own voice played back from the recording, it will sound to him like the voice of someone else. Some whose voices have been recorded without their knowledge have failed to recognize them when they heard them played back. The preacher who will take such a recording of his voice and study it carefully as it is played over to him a number of times will hear defects of which he had been completely unaware. If it is impossible to make a recording of an entire message in connection with a radio broadcast, much can be accomplished in listening to even an eight- or ten-inch record on which has been recorded merely the recitation of a poem or a passage of Scripture or a few words spoken extemporaneously or a brief paragraph from a sermon. Firms which do this type of recording will be found in every large city; but even a home recording or dictaphone cylinder, though the tone quality is not so good nor the reproduction so accurate, will afford considerable help to the preacher who wishes to overcome bad habits of speech.

X

THE PREACHER IN THE PULPIT

BY HIS PULPIT PERSONALITY we mean the impression a preacher makes personally upon those who sit in his audience as he occupies the pulpit.

Is it any concern of the preacher's what men think of him? Is it not his business to make them think well of his Lord and not of himself? Is it right for him to be concerned about the personal impression that he makes? Certainly the preacher has no right to be concerned primarily with what his hearers think of him. He should be very much concerned with what they think of his Lord through him. It is his duty to glorify God by being as attractive a representative of his Lord as it is possible for him to be. Certainly the preacher should "hide behind the cross." Men should be so occupied with his message that they become unconscious of him, but an attractive personality will win men to the hearing of His words and the preacher will be forgotten as he loses himself in his preaching. Nothing makes it so difficult for a listener to forget the speaker and concentrate upon his message as unpleasant traits of personality. They intrude themselves like distracting noises upon the clear music of the Gospel.

The purpose of a lighthouse is to attract attention to itself that men may become conscious of the message the lighthouse is placed to convey. Men see the lighthouse and are warned of dangerous rocks. They are attracted by its beam and find the channel. They forget the beauty and the brilliance of the light as they become concerned with its message and its warning. The light is most brilliant and beautiful as it passes through a perfect lens. The preacher whose light shines out through an attractive personality best accomplishes the task for which God has placed him in the pulpit. The sincere preacher should be vitally concerned about developing such a personality, not to make men conscious of his winsomeness that he may enjoy their admiration, but that he may accomplish the purpose for which God has set him like a lighthouse in the darkness of the world—the purpose of warning men of the danger of the rocks of sin and of guiding them to Christ.

The preacher is the representative of the Lord Jesus Christ, the most attractive personality that ever graced the earth. It is the preacher's responsibility to represent his Lord fairly and as a good ambassador he should seek to develop a personality which is winsome and attractive. It is not in the compass of this book to discuss personality generally, but the question of pulpit personality is a vital part of any work on pulpit speech. There are some men whose personality in the pulpit is entirely different from their personality out of the pulpit. There are those who on the platform present a sweet and winsome manner but who, in personal contact, are most unattractive. Their personalities are like those oil paintings which are lovely when viewed from a distance and in the proper light, but which when seen close up present only a muddle of color. Possibly the difference in their pulpit and out-of-the-pulpit personalities is due to the fact that in the pulpit they make an effort to be winsome, while in private life they simply do not bother. It is possible that out of sheer vanity a man will wish to appear in public in the best light possible, while in private life he is too selfish or too lazy to make himself agreeable to his intimates. There are preachers whose congregations find them most attractive but whose wives deserve sympathy. There are some preachers who are most forceful and impelling in the pulpit, whose selfishness and bad manners at the dinner table make them obnoxious to those who have to eat with them. Of course, not only every preacher but also every Christian should seek for the sake of his Christian testimony to cultivate a personality which will attract men all the time, and it is to be doubted that a man can permanently manifest a winsome personality in the pulpit who has not cultivated qualities of character which will make him attractive when he meets people face to face and rubs shoulders with them in private life, since sometimes under the pressure of special stress or irritation he will forget this pulpit manner in the pulpit.

There are certain definite qualities which go to make up attractive pulpit personality. A man may possess one or more of these characteristics—he may even combine them all and still not have a pleasant personality. However, no personality can be pleasant without them.

Nothing takes the place of sincerity in the pulpit. A man may be wise and well trained. He may possess all the technical facility which a public speaker can acquire, but if his sermons do not spring from deep-seated personal conviction, if he has chosen the ministry from selfish motives and without a sense of a divine call, he can never hope to beget confidence in his hearers. It may be possible that an insincere man will be acceptable to his hearers for a little while, but there is something about insincerity which people can detect. A man may not be able to put his finger on the trouble but he will instinctively come to feel as he sits under the ministry of an insincere preacher that there is something wrong somewhere.

It is not enough to be just sincere. A man may be entirely sincere and be a failure as a preacher, but no man was ever a success in the ministry who was not a sincere man. You cannot expect people to believe you if you are not yourself convinced. You have no right to expect their confidence if insincerity on your part makes you unworthy of it. The preacher should live a life that inspires confidence. His personal relationships should be above reproach. In the pulpit he should never be guilty of saying for effect something which he knows is not true. It is not always wise to be completely frank. It is sometimes a mark both of wisdom and of spiritual apprehension to keep silent, but when the preacher does speak, he should speak what he believes to be the truth and what he knows to be his personal conviction.

A good preacher is interested in his people. The pastor should be devoted to his flock. He should feel responsible for their spiritual welfare. He should be genuinely touched with their sorrows and share with them in their joys, and no man can be a successful pastor who does not possess such interest and devotion. It is not enough to speak hollow words of congratulations or sympathy. To be effective, such words must spring from deep impulses and not from a sense of duty. A preacher must be capable of deep feeling. He must possess a sympathetic heart. He must have an understanding of grief and a compassion for human sorrow. He must sympathize with suffering. He must know human nature well enough to feel no surprise at sin and to put no confidence in the flesh, but at the same time he must deal with the sinner as one who considers himself, lest he also be tempted. There must be a sincere desire to help in time of need, a sincere willingness to give one's self. Above all, there must be a sincere passion for souls, a genuine desire to bring men and women into a saving knowledge of the Lord Jesus Christ.

There must be no show, no pretense, no hypocrisy. The preacher in the pulpit should be what he is. He should not attempt to appear wiser or more virtuous, more scholarly, or more spiritual.

"But," you may ask, "is sincerity necessary to an at-

91

tractive personality in the pulpit? May not a man pretend something which he does not feel and by so doing make his personality more winsome?" Not in the pulpit. An actor on the stage may assume a part in which he expresses opinions he does not hold and pretend emotions which he does not feel. In private life he may be an individual of most unattractive personality, yet seem on the stage to be quite lovable. The audience considers the character in the drama apart from the personal life of the man who acts the part. It is an actor's business to pretend and a good actor goes sincerely about the business of pretense. He is sincere and conscientious in doing the thing he is supposed to do, the thing the audience has paid to see him do. The actor is not insincere. He seeks to portray honestly the emotions of the character whom the dramatist has created. He is an artist practising his profession. There is no comparison between the actor before his audience and the preacher called of God who stands in front of a congregation to open to them the divine Word. The preacher's business is to declare what he himself sincerely believes to be the mind of God. There is no place for the make-believe here. No fable is being unfolded, no thin-spun thread of dramatic plot unraveled. Eternal destinies are at stake. Hungry-hearted men do not go to church for an hour of entertainment. They come for divine certainties. If they detect any measure of insincerity in the preacher, his pulpit personality is bad.

The second essential of a good pulpit personality is naturalness. Naturalness and sincerity are closely related but not identical. A man may be perfectly sincere and so unnatural that he gives the impression of insincerity. Sincerity is freedom from pretense: naturalness is freedom from artificiality. Preacher, be yourself in the pulpit! An unnatural tone of voice or manner of speaking can mar an otherwise pleasant pulpit personality. "Well," some men will say, "if personality depends upon speaking and acting in my own way, why should I bother to study pulpit behaviour and speech?" Why is a diamond polished? Not to make it seem like something else than a diamond, but to bring out the beauty and the luster hidden in the uncut and unpolished stone. To refuse to train one's self to speak properly for fear of becoming unnatural is as stupid as refusing to educate a child for fear of his becoming conceited. Just as the ignorant man is sometimes the most conceited man, so the preacher without training is sometimes the most unnatural in the pulpit. Training brings confidence, ease, and facility. It is difficult for a man to be natural in the pulpit who feels self-conscious, uncomfortable, and awkward.

Unnaturalness often springs from imitation. It is every man's privilege to train and use in his own way the gifts and talents which God has given him. Mannerisms and peculiarities of speech which are effective in the man with whom they are natural are ridiculous when imitated. Every preacher should develop his own style. He should *develop* it but be sure to keep it his *own*. An original style full of imperfections is infinitely better than a perfect style which is imitated. The most effective manner of speaking which a man can use in the pulpit is his own manner. Of course, he should try to remove the flaws and defects. He should so educate himself that the use of good English becomes natural with him, but the literary style, the organization of his ideas —these should be his own and they should be delivered in his own voice, not in imitation of someone else's voice.

The most effective public delivery has its model in a man's natural conversational style. The purpose of voice development and training as emphasized in Chapter IX is not to give a man a different voice and manner of speaking in the pulpit from those which he uses out of the pulpit. It is to help him realize the full potentialities of his voice which should not be neglected, either in private conversation or in the pulpit. Pulpit speech should be simply an enlargement of the conversational speech. A small picture is not effective from a distance. To be seen by a crowd it must be enlarged. The composition of the picture is not changed in the process of enlargement but certain details are more apparent in the large picture than in the small one. When a trained speaker gets up to preach, he does not change his voice and style of speech. He simply enlarges it. He is still himself. He is natural, but it is a naturalness which is attractive because it is the result of study and training—of culture and proper development.

The third essential to a good pulpit personality is "bigness." The preacher should be free from personal animosities, jealousies, ill-will, petulence, spite, and meanness. Just to the extent that a man is filled with these impulses just to that extent is his personality marred. A "big" man has conviction. A "little" man has prejudices which he calls convictions and carries like chips on his shoulder. The man who is controlled by base ambition and little ugly human impulses will evidence his smallness when he stands in the pulpit to declare the truths of God. The man who would be free from these impulses must be controlled and dominated by the Holy Spirit. His power in the life evidences itself in kindliness and sweetness of personality when the preacher stands before his congregation, but it is a kindness which does not condone sin. It is not a superficial kindness like that of the father who allows a child to go unpunished because he hates to give him a moment of pain or unhappiness. It is the sort of kindness which lashes out against sin because sin injures men, but it is a kindness which seeks to reach the sinner. The sweetness is not sticky and effeminate, expressing itself in shallow platitudes and vague nothings. It is a masculine sweetness, strong but gentle.

Dress and Physical Appearance

In connection with personality something should be said about appearance and dress. Though a dynamic personality may overcome a bad impression created by physical appearance, few men are dynamic enough to overcome such a handicap. Even a minister endowed with the strongest and

94

most attractive personality will find that proper care in the matter of his personal appearance in the pulpit will be an asset in his dealing with the audience and increase the respect of his people for him and strengthen his leadership.

A minister should not seem to give undue consideration to his appearance. Neither should he give the impression of being totally unconcerned with it. It should go without saying that his hair should be well combed, his face clean, his teeth brushed, his shirt immaculate, his clothes well pressed and free from spots, and his shoes shined.

Out of the pulpit there is no reason why a preacher should dress differently from men in other professions, nor why he should confine himself exclusively to dark suits and dull ties. He should dress as becomes a professional man of his age. In the pulpit for a formal Sunday service he should be conservatively dressed. In some city pulpits it is customary for the minister to wear morning clothes for the Sunday morning worship hour. In other churches it is the custom for the minister to go even further and wear a pulpit gown. Generally, however, for the average church a dark suit of conservative cut is appropriate. In any case, a white shirt should be worn. The tie should be of conservative pattern—solid black is always safe, or black or navy blue with a thin white stripe—and black socks and black shoes are in order unless the preacher is dressed in a dark brown suit, in which case a dark brown or wine-colored tie, and dark brown shoes and socks should be worn. For the pulpit a dark blue or oxford gray suit is a little more formal than the dark brown and possibly more appropriate. A young preacher should not attempt to dress like an old man. His clothes, both in pattern and in cut, need not be so conservative as those of an older man. In hot weather a white suit is generally acceptable, even for a Sunday morning service, and always so in the evening. Extremes of dress and flashy personal idiosyncrasies in clothes are to be avoided. For special services during the week, Bible conferences, evangelistic meetings, etc., a business suit of lighter color may be acceptable, and if it is an informal occasion the preacher may even wear a colored shirt. However, a white shirt is always preferable. The preacher should consider the occasion and the place in the matter of dress for these special meetings. Conservative congregations in certain sections of the country would be shocked if a preacher ever ascended their pulpit in a light suit, even for a special informal midweek service. The same congregation would, however, think nothing of his appearing in the parish house or Sunday school auditorium in light clothes for the same type of service. A preacher is wise not to offend the sensibilities of his congregation or to violate too radically the established custom. A visiting preacher will do well to consult the pastor about the custom of the local church and the attitude of the people.

There will be some occasions on which the preacher who looks unlike the popular conception of a preacher can accomplish more for the Lord than the man who fits the popular picture. This is particularly true when speaking to high school assemblies, groups of prisoners, and soldiers. There are other times when the more a preacher fits in appearance the popular conception of a minister, the more acceptable his message will be. The preacher should, therefore, consider also the audience as well as the occasion and place in the matter of selecting his wardrobe.

There are some people who feel that a preacher should not be concerned about his clothes, that when he finds himself decently covered he has given as much concern as a preacher should to the matter of dress. To occupy oneself further, they feel, is vanity and worldliness. Such is not the case. If a salesman is careful of his appearance, should not a preacher be? If the businessman seeks to make a good impression in the interest of his business, should not also the minister make like effort in the interest of the Gospel? Anything which affects his ministry should be a vital concern of the minister. The man who neglects his personal appearance reflects upon his calling. The preacher in the pulpit is, as Sam Jones discovered while sitting under the ministry of Simeon Peter Richardson, not a prisoner but a king; the pulpit is not a prison but a throne. Harm may be done to the cause of Christ by the grease spots on the well-rounded front of a preacher's vest. There have been conscientious preachers who would have been wiser and have accomplished more in their ministry if they had taken a little time from the preparation of the message and arrangement of the notes to prepare their own appearance and arrange their apparel. Certainly a preacher should not be extravagant in his dress. The average preacher cannot afford an extensive wardrobe or fine clothes. If he could afford them, it would be wrong for him to spend money extravagantly upon himself. Not much money but much care should be spent upon the preacher's clothes. They should be wisely chosen and kept clean and in press.

Before he goes into the pulpit, the preacher should see that his tie is in place, that it is properly tied, that the knot is tight enough so that it will not slip. If there is a handkerchief in his breast pocket he should be sure it is clean and that just enough of it shows. From the moment he enters the pulpit he should seem unconscious of his clothes.

Cleanliness

But it is not enough for a preacher to look clean. He should smell clean. The physical exertion and nervous strain of preaching will make him perspire. He may have just stepped out of his bath, dressed and entered the pulpit, but unless he has used a deodorant the chances are that by the time the service is over he will be in no condition for close contact with people in the confines of a small room. The considerate man will slip a breath tablet, a peppermint, or a clove into his mouth before he shakes hands with people after a service, and he will not eat onions before doing personal work and dealing with penitents.

97

On entering the pulpit, the conscientious preacher will feel the need of calling upon the Lord. He will feel the awful responsibility of preaching. He will have a sense of his own weakness and impotence. He will feel the need of divine infilling. He will seek to be led by the Holy Spirit. To the man whose ministry is blessed of God preaching never becomes commonplace. Luther said, "Although I am old and experienced in speaking, I tremble whenever I ascend the pulpit." No man is worthy of preaching who does not approach his preaching with somewhat the same feeling.

It is the practice of some men to kneel on entering the pulpit. Others pray while seated, simply bowing the head upon the hand. Whichever is the preacher's custom, whichever he feels led to do, whichever he can do with least self-consciousness—this is the method he should follow. Having cast himself upon the Lord and sought divine leading in the service, the preacher will enter with reverence and dignity into the public worship. A preacher makes a poor impression who laughs and talks with another minister in the pulpit during the instrumental prelude, offertory or any other part of the service.

It is a good practice while seated in the pulpit during the playing of the prelude to look over the congregation. To ignore them altogether and avoid looking at them at all conveys an impression of coldness and indifference. Glance over the entire congregation in such a way that each person present will feel that you have seen him. Do not greet each individual with a glance. Simply let the people making up your congregation know you are conscious of their presence. This moment of looking at your audience will establish a contact between pulpit and pew even before you stand up to address them. If you are a stranger in the church, a visiting minister or a new pastor, whom many of the congregation are seeing for the first time, it is more than ever important that you establish this feeling. But do not seem to be counting the congregation!

The preacher's manner in the pulpit should be natural and unaffected. He should not be long-faced. He should be careful not to look harsh. His glance should be friendly and open. There is no reason why a preacher should appear lugubrious and sad every time he goes into the pulpit, and he should not take with him there in the expression of his countenance a trace of personal problems or of any unpleasantness with which he may have been faced. He enters the pulpit as God's messenger. He comes to declare the truth of God's Word and the freedom and joy in Christ Jesus. He should be free from self-consciousness. He should be concerned with his message. His manner of worship should be reverent, his attitude toward the congregation dignified but gracious.

A preacher should be careful to maintain an attitude of dignity in the pulpit. For a certain type service—for example, Sunday evening worship or evening evangelistic services—he may be informal. He should never be undignified. There should never be anything in his manner which suggests a lack of realization of responsibility toward his ministry. He should seem at ease, and should give the impression of being at home in the pulpit, of being familiar with the business of directing a service; but he should never let these become commonplace to him or his manner will be lacking in dignity and reverence. Sir James Stonhouse, who became one of the most gracious and forceful preachers of his day, once had David Garrick, the actor, in his congregation. After the service the actor asked Dr. Stonhouse what particular business he had to perform when the service was over.

"None," said the other.

"I thought you had," said Garrick, "on seeing you enter the reading-desk in such a hurry. Nothing can be more indecent than to see a clergyman set about sacred business as if he were a tradesman, and go into the church as if he wanted to get out of it as soon as possible." He next asked the doctor what books he had before him.

"Only the Bible and Prayer Book."

"Only the Bible and Prayer Book?" replied the player, "why, you tossed them backwards and forwards, and turned the leaves as carelessly, as if they were those of a daybook and ledger." *

The doctor acknowledged the force of the criticism by henceforth avoiding the faults it was designed to correct. Might not many a young preacher of our own day wisely profit by the same?

XI

CONDUCTING THE
FORMAL WORSHIP SERVICE

THOUGH THE SERMON is the very center and most important part of a service, it is, after all, only a part. A congregation assembles in the house of the Lord on Sunday morning to worship God as well as to be instructed from His Word. All too often preachers have a tendency to look upon all of the service except the sermon as of little importance. Too often the hymns and prayer and reading of the Scripture which proceed the sermon are referred to disparagingly as the "preliminaries." They are not the preliminaries. They are a portion of the service, and an important portion. They serve to prepare the minds and hearts of the hearers for the sermon, but they do much more than this. They afford the congregation an opportunity for active participation in the public worship of God. In hymns and prayer God is

* Mrs. Helen C. Knight, *Lady Huntington and Her Friends* (New York: American Tract Society, 1853), pp. 80-81.

praised and honored and the blessing of His presence and power in the service is sought. Great attention and careful consideration should be given, therefore, to the planning of the entire service.

The Order of Worship

The various Protestant denominations suggest certain orders of worship for the use of their ministers. In most cases, however, the preacher is at liberty to alter such a form of service or to depart from the suggested routine as he feels led or as his taste dictates. There are, of course, certain churches—the Episcopalian, for example—which use a liturgical service more or less fixed and prescribed. Here are some suggested orders of worship which are suitable for a non-liturgical service:

A. First form
    I. Doxology
    II. Invocation
    III. Hymn of praise
    IV. Reading of Scripture
    V. Pastoral prayer
    VI. Announcements and offertory
    VII. Offertory anthem
    VIII. A hymn
    IX. Sermon
    X. Closing hymn
    XI. Benediction

B. Second form
    I. Organ prelude
    II. Doxology
    III. Pastoral call to worship
    IV. Invocation and Lord's Prayer
    V. Anthem
    VI. Scripture lesson
    VII. Hymn of praise
    VIII. Pastoral prayer
    IX. Announcements

X. Hymn of devotion
XI. Offertory prayer
XII. Offertory solo
XIII. Sermon
XIV. Prayer
XV. Hymn
XVI. Benediction
XVII. Postlude

C. Third form
I. Organ prelude
II. Doxology
III. Pastoral call to worship
IV. Anthem
V. Hymn
VI. Apostles' creed
VII. Scripture lesson
VIII. Prayer
IX. Announcements
X. Hymn
XI. Offertory prayer
XII. Offertory solo
XIII. Sermon
XIV. Prayer
XV. Hymn
XVI. Benediction
XVII. Postlude

D. Fourth form
I. Hymn of praise
II. Invocation
III. Responsive reading
IV. Hymn
V. Prayer
VI. Announcements and offertory
VII. Sermon
VIII. Closing prayer
IX. Closing hymn
X. Benediction

It will be noted that in the last suggested form there is no provision made for a special number by the choir and it is suggested for churches without a choir. It will be further noted that in all four of the suggested forms of worship there are three hymns included. Such should be, as a general rule, the *minimum* number used at a formal Sunday service.

Selection and Announcements of Hymns

Care should be given to the selection of the hymns. The minister should bear in mind the theme of the morning message, the purpose of each hymn and the place in the service where it will be used (and, of course, he should take into consideration any special occasion of worship such as Christmas, Thanksgiving, New Year's, or Easter). We do not mean to imply by this that all the hymns should have a direct bearing upon the theme of the morning discourse, though as a general rule at least one, either the second or the last, and perhaps both of these, should be in line with the theme of the message.

The first hymn should always be a hymn of praise, thanksgiving, and adoration, or one that stresses the greatness of God as demonstrated in some attribute of Deity or evidenced in nature and creation, or it should express a call to worship or invoke the presence of God upon the assembly. This hymn should always be lofty and noble in sentiment and of a cheerful mood. "When Morning Gilds the Skies," "O Could I Speak the Matchless Worth," "All Hail the Power of Jesus' Name," are examples of praise hymns. "Come, Holy Spirit, Heavenly Dove," and "Come, Thou Fount of Every Blessing," are examples of the invocation type of hymn. "Holy, Holy, Holy," "A Mighty Fortress is Our God," "The Spacious Firmament on High," are examples of hymns dealing with the power and attributes of Deity which are appropriate for opening the worship service.

The hymn near the center of the service may be one of several types. It may be purely devotional in character, such as, "Jesus, the Very Thought of Thee," or "Jesus, Thou Joy of Loving Heart." It may, if just preceding the offertory, be an offertory hymn such as Dykes' "O Lord of Heaven and Earth and Sea." This second hymn, when it comes just before the sermon, may be in line with the theme of the message in order to prepare the hearts of the congregation for the sermon. Or, again, it may be a hymn imploring the blessing of the Lord upon the message as it is delivered. Such a hymn is "Break Thou the Bread of Life," and "Lord, We Come before Thee Now." A hymn of praise is also appropriate for use as the second hymn of the service.

The closing hymn may fix the "appeal" of the sermon in the mind of the congregation; it may be an invitation hymn or a hymn of consecration; or it may be simply one of dismissal and benediction, such as "Lord, Dismiss Us with Thy Blessing," or "Oh, Saviour, Bless Us ere We Go."

It will be noticed that all the hymns referred to as examples are "formal" in type. It is for that very reason they are appropriate for a formal service of worship. There are excellent hymns less formal in style which have a useful and appropriate place, but it is not the formal Sunday morning worship service. There are songs intended for evangelistic meetings, and others which are intended for Sunday school or for an informal evening service, when it is the custom of the church not to have a formal service on Sunday night but rather an evangelistic service. Such hymns and songs are inappropriate for a formal Sunday morning period of worship. Fine old hymns of Watts, and Wesley, of Cowper, and Doddridge, or Horatius Bonar and Martin Luther, are worshipful in character and most of them are "sound" in doctrine and of excellent literary value. They not only furnish inspiration to worship and an avenue of expression for praise and prayer, but have a cultural value also. One of the saddest tendencies of our day in Christian circles is the neglect of the old hymns and the increasing use of "shallow" songs and particularly of the finical choruses so popular, particularly among young people. While there

are a *few* of these choruses which are Scriptural and have
some doctrinal, literary, or musical value, the great majority
of them are frivolous, light, sentimental, of poor literary
quality, and of little musical value.

A pastor owes it to his flock to make them familiar with
the grand and majestic hymns of the church by using them
regularly on Sunday morning. He should himself be familiar with the great hymns and should not hesitate from
time to time to include in his Sunday morning service one
with which the congregation may not be so familiar but with
which they should become familiar. It will lend interest
and variety if the preacher will occasionally in introducing
such a hymn say a few words about it or its author and how
it came to be written. He may refer to the truth presented
in the hymn by quoting some verse of Scripture, and then
by a reading of the hymn aloud before it is sung point up
the parallel between the Scripture and the thought expressed
by the hymn writer.

Many excellent books on hymnology are available. Every
preacher's library should contain at least one, so that he
himself may increase his own knowledge of the hymns and
of the stories behind them, and thus be able occasionally to
present such material to his people in order to increase their
appreciation of the hymns and to fix the thought and message of the verses in their minds as they sing them.

The preacher should announce his hymns in as varied a
way as possible, and should be careful not to fall into the
habit of using the same phrase of announcement over and
over again. The number of the hymn should be announced
carefully and clearly at least twice. It is a good idea to give
the number of the hymn at the beginning of the announcement of it and again at the close of the announcement. For
example:

"Hymn number 303. (Three hundred three. Never three
hundred *and* three.) Nowhere is the joy and triumph of
surrender to God better expressed than in this hymn of

George Mattias. "O Love that will not let me go" is a hymn so familiar there is danger of our singing the words without regard for their meaning. I hope that today this will be more to us than a hymn thoughtlessly sung. Number 303."

Again, for variety's sake the preacher may simply announce the number of the hymn and have it sung without further comment.

FORMS OF PUBLIC PRAYER

There is always a grave danger in laying down certain rules for the form and construction of a prayer, for in attempting to follow the rules one is liable to become so involved in the "making" of a prayer that he will forget that he is supposed to be *praying* one. Any preacher should receive a compliment on the beauty of his prayer with heart-searching. There is no reason why a prayer should not be beautiful. In fact, there is every reason why it should be, but the hearers, if they are in the proper spirit of devotion, and the preacher, if he is pouring out his heart to God, should both have their thoughts fixed upon praise and petition and not upon the way in which praise and petition are being expressed.

However, there are certain suggestions which can be profitably followed in the organization and utterance of the public prayer in order to assure the proper attitude of worship and reverence and to avoid "vain repetition."

The minister should bear in mind that when he leads a congregation in prayer he is not praying for himself alone, but for the entire group. He should, therefore, avoid the use of the singular personal pronoun, both in the nominative and objective cases. It should not be "Bless me as I bring the message this morning," but rather, "Use Thy servant in the preaching of Thy Word this day." It should go without saying, of course, that when a minister is leading a congregation in prayer they are entitled to hear what he is saying. A man should never pray *to* his congregation, but since they are supposed to be praying with him, they should hear clearly the words which he is addressing to the Lord. The minister in the pulpit is supposed to be the voice giving expression to the praise and petition of the entire group.

The repetition of any stock phrase of address to the Deity should be avoided, as also such phrases as "We Pray Thee," "Oh, we beseech Thee," "We ask Thee," etc. Most preachers are guilty of one or the other or both of these faults.

Custom, fostered no doubt by the use of the King James' version of the Bible, with its old English forms, decrees the use of *Thee, Thou, Thy,* and *Thine* when addressing the Deity. The modern forms, *you* and *yours,* customary in conversational use, are improper for public prayer. The proper corresponding old English form of the verb *to be* as the predicate should follow when *Thou* is the subject, as: "Thou art," "Thou wast," etc. The same is true of the verb *to do* and *to will.* The proper form, for example, is "Thou dost" and "Wilt Thou?" However, in phrases of entreaty the modern form *do* is acceptable as, "Do Thou undertake for us, O Lord." In such cases, however, the phrase is generally stronger if the *do Thou* is omitted altogether and a direct entreaty used, as: "Undertake for us, O Lord."

A definite reverence should be maintained. No man has a right to come carelessly into the presence of God. We are invited to "come *boldly* unto the throne of Grace," but we must not come *presumptuously* there. Every minister should evidence a deep and personal relationship with God in his prayers from the pulpit, but no man should manifest familiarity toward God.

The way to acquire ease and propriety in public prayer without having to give conscious attention to such things is to practice these principles in one's private devotions until they become natural. Broadus calls attention to the fact that if preaching is the way to learn how to preach, certainly praying is necessary if one is to learn how to pray. It is a point well made.

There will be, as a general rule, at least two and possibly three prayers in the average worship service. The invocation used toward the beginning of the service is, as the name indicates, an invoking, that is, a prayer for the presence of God in the service and for His blessing upon it. Though such a prayer may also contain a petition for the preparation of the hearts of the people, or include a phrase or two of praise and adoration, such as "Just and holy is Thy name, O Lord," or "The earth is the Lord's and the fulness thereof," this prayer is usually quite brief.

The regular morning prayer, oftentimes called the *pastoral prayer,* comes later in the service and is considerably more lengthy. Such a prayer should not be made up of stereotyped phrases, but there should be a certain definite order and arrangement so that the preacher will not pray around in a circle and neglect some particular matter that should be the object of prayer. It is well, therefore, that he give some thought in advance to the petitions which are appropriate for the occasion and for the subject of his sermon. The arrangement which is most generally followed is: first, the address to Deity, invocation, and thanksgiving; second, a general confession of sin; third, intercession. The particular items of intercession are the chief points to which thought should be given in advance. Of course, there are certain general matters which should not be neglected, though each cannot be mentioned every Sunday. Such objects of intercession are missionaries, the sick, the lonely, those members of the congregation who are away (not, of course, mentioning them by name), those in sorrow or illness (in such cases it is customary in some churches when prayer has been requested for certain individuals to mention them by name), and Christian colleges, Bible institutes, etc.

This prayer should not be of undue length. It may be longer when the congregation is seated or kneeling than when they are standing. It should, as all public prayers, be prayed simply and forcefully in a natural tone of voice, not rushed or hurried.

The third prayer which may be included in a service of worship is the closing prayer. This may be omitted and the benediction used alone, or the closing prayer may come just after the sermon, before the announcement of the final hymn, with the benediction at the close of the hymn; or the prayer may be used after the hymn and conclude with the benediction. It may be a prayer of consecration, a petition that the truths acquired may remain in the minds and produce results in the lives of the hearers, or it may be a request for blessing and peace upon the congregation.

READING THE SCRIPTURE

The public reading of the Word of God is a vital part of the service, yet there is no other portion so often performed badly or passed over casually.

To read the Scripture publicly and do a good job of it requires time, thought, and effort. Only one who is willing to make diligent preparation and to spend hours of practice at it can learn to read the Bible aloud forcefully and effectively. Having once acquired the art, he should still spend some time in careful study of the portion which he is to read on a specific occasion.

Of course, he must acquire a proper knowledge of the pronunciation of both the ordinary words and of the proper names of the Bible. But there is more to public reading of the Scriptures than pronouncing the words carefully and accurately.

There must also be proper emphasis, expression, and force; and no one can learn to read the Scripture with proper emphasis and expression and force who cannot read easily. To be an effective reader one should be able to read at least two lines or more at a glance. In this way he is able to grasp the thought of the entire phrase or sentence and begin his reading of it with the proper emphasis and inflection necessary to convey the meaning of the whole phrase or sentence. Entirely too many people have been taught to read a word at a time rather than to read by thoughts, and they have acquired certain bad habits as a result. When they read aloud every word stands out by itself. It is a case of: *The Lord is my shepherd*. One of the best ways to overcome this habit of word-reading is to go through a passage and underline the important words, using a double line under the most important, and crossing out letters not pronounced, and then reading the passage over and over again aloud. This will not, however, in itself completely overcome the trouble. One must learn to pronounce certain small words, particularly articles, prepositions, and conjunctions, not as they are spelled but as they are pronounced in ordinary conversation. *The* is ~~thē~~ before a word beginning with a consonant, but before a word beginning with a vowel it is ~~thĕ~~. The article *a* is nearly always unstressed. One does not say, Ā MAN, but *à* MAN. *To* is generally in conversation *tŭ*, not *tōo*. One must learn to give these words the same sort of treatment in reading that they receive in good, ordinary speech.

Having mastered the mere technical matters essential to reading with smoothness and a natural quality, one then comes up against the problem of learning to read with proper expression in order to convey the meaning and mood of a passage. A good rule to follow in the reading of Scripture is this: Read the passage just as you would read any similar passage from another type of literature. Of course, the Bible as the Word of God should be treated with more reverence than is attached to any book of human authorship. However, the Book is vital and alive and should be publicly read as living literature, not in the cold, dead, stilted fashion which so many clergymen, particularly the well-trained clergymen of certain liturgical groups, affect for the reading of God's Word.

There are many types of literature in the Bible. Poetry is found in the Psalms and in certain other passages. History is found in the Pentateuch and the Gospels. "Mystical" literature is represented by the prophetic books, some of it couched in a poetic prose. Discussions of doctrine and conduct are found, for example, in the Epistles. There are also narratives on various levels of dramatic excitement, philosophical discussions, and legal phrases. Each type of literature requires a treatment somewhat different from that given to any other.

Having determined under what type of literature the passage selected for reading may be classified, it is then a good policy to read the passage through simply for the meaning. One then studies the passage to determine the points of climax and the points of least importance, that he may give them the proper relative emphasis in reading. Having fixed these firmly in mind, one should next read for color and variety. These are acquired in oral reading by the use of the same technical principles which make for variety in speaking: pitch, progress, punch, and pause.

It is advisable next to read aloud in an effort to convey the "mood" and "feeling" of the passage. Certain portions of God's Word are sad and solemn; others are filled with overflowing joy, breaking forth in praise; some portions are quiet and placid; others are turbulent. Some portions are simple and "homey" in mood; others are eloquent and highly dramatic. This characteristic mood should be expressed in the voice when the passage is read. One should be careful, however, while maintaining the basic mood, to achieve the variety necessary if monotony is to be avoided and the interest of the listeners held throughout the portion.

There is no doubt that it is more difficult to read the Bible aloud than most other literature. The Bible, at least in the versions commonly used, is in an English that is archaic and decidedly different from the language of our common speech. The divisions of the various books of the Bible into chapters and verses also add to the difficulties of interpreting the meaning properly when reading it aloud. Chapter and verse divisions are not inspired. They have been put in by translators and editors. Many ministers read the Bible as if the divisions were inspired, even to the point of stopping completely at the end of each verse, although oftentimes that means stopping in the middle of a thought. As a matter of fact, sometimes to stop *at the end of a chapter* is to stop with an incomplete or undeveloped thought set forth.

One who finds difficulty in learning to read the Scripture easily and to catch its full meaning will find it helpful to type off the portion which is to be read without any division into verses, paragraphing it according to thoughts as any good modern English prose would be paragraphed. If he will practice reading from this transcribed copy he will find it is much easier to interpret the exact meaning of the passage than when he reads it directly from the Bible, where it is divided into verses. When the time comes to read the passage publicly from the Word of God, he should disregard the divisions entirely and read the passage as he read it from the paragraphed copy.

Too much cannot be said about the importance of proper and meaningful reading of the Bible in the hearing of the congregation. Effectively and reverently read, it will be a high point of beauty in the service, for it is His Word, which God has promised to bless; it is His Word, which is "forever fixed in heaven." To read it carelessly, to rush through it, to mangle it or read it unintelligently is inexcusable.

XII

RADIO PREACHING

WHEN ONE CONSIDERS the scores of sermons now broadcast each day these words written in 1879 seem strangely humorous:

"The Spirit of God employs not only the truth, but the utmost power of utterance, intonation, countenance, and gesticulation. I think Dr. Dick first suggested that the time might come when the preacher could sit in his study, and, by means of tubes properly arranged, could address a distant congregation. A similar use has been suggested for the telephone. While either of these processes would convey the sound to the ear with the accent and intonation of the speaker, who does not feel that by such a process the chief power and influence of the pulpit would be lost? Were not the presence of the preacher necessary, God could have employed the ministry of angels, or each person might have been addressed by a vision or a voice." *

Radio affords the richest opportunity of our day to reach the greatest number of people with the Gospel, and since many preachers have regular radio programs and since almost every preacher will have some occasion to broadcast, a discussion of the radio sermon and of broadcasting technique comes well within the scope of a book which deals with the subject of preaching.

As has been suggested, a preacher does well to consider the type of audience to which his message is addressed. No visible congregation is ever so varied or conglomerate as the great mass of listeners who hear a single broadcast. A radio audience is composed of men, women, and children of all classes, ranges of intelligence, and degrees of education. A radio preacher speaks to members of his own denomination and of practically every other denomination, as well as to Jews and Catholics. While the size and location of the station and the hour of the day have some effect upon the type of audience, no broadcast can be addressed to any single group. During the day, particularly in the forenoon, surveys have revealed, a large portion of a radio audience is made up of women who keep the radio turned on as they go about their housekeeping duties. In the evenings and on Sundays a great many more men will be listening than dur-

* Matthew Simpson, *Lectures on Preaching* (New York: Phillips & Hunt, 1879), p. 167.

ing a week day. Meal times are especially good for programs addressed to the family as a whole. Naturally a large and more powerful station will reach farther than a small station, both because it has a coverage of greater area and because the large stations are generally located in metropolitan districts. The smaller stations usually have a higher proportion of rural listeners.

On a small station located in a town in the midst of a farming area for a morning broadcast intended to reach the family as it sits about the breakfast table, it is advisable to select a very early hour as country families are early risers. On a larger station or one located in a city of considerable size a program an hour or two later will be more likely to reach the greatest number of listening families around breakfast time. People dwelling in rural territories retire earlier than city people, and so an evening broadcast addressed largely to rural listeners should be put on the air earlier than one intended primarily for an urban audience.

A preacher may be called upon to take part in one of two types of broadcasts. An entire service may be picked up by remote control and broadcast directly from the auditorium of his church or he may take part in a broadcast originating from the studio. The technique of these two different types of broadcasts is entirely different. In the church service the preacher's chief obligation is to the congregation in front of him. The regular service should be conducted as is customary; some concessions should be made, however, to the radio audience. Long pauses should be avoided, the whole progress of the service should be "tightened" somewhat so that there will not be moments of silence, as, for example, between the announcement of the hymn and the beginning of the instrumental introduction to the hymn. There can be no pause while the preacher turns through the Bible to find his text or while he adjusts his glasses or arranges his notes before beginning to speak. The congregation in the church auditorium will know what is occurring during these silences; radio listeners will not know and such pauses will either cause them to lose interest and tune the program out or at least break the mood of concentration upon the service.

If a pause is necessary, as, for example, while the ushers are bringing the offering forward, it should be covered by soft music of the organ or the piano.

At a regular church service which is being broadcast the minister should preach to his congregation. The radio audience realizes it is listening to the broadcast of a regular service from a church auditorium and the listeners by exercise of their imagination will project themselves into the service. As a rule, it is bad technique to address the radio audience exclusively, even for a few moments in the course of a sermon, and in so doing ignore the visible congregation. This does not mean, however, that special announcements cannot be addressed to the radio listeners or that they cannot be included in remarks made. For example, the preacher may make an announcement in the following fashion: "Those who worship with us as the program is broadcast to them this morning will be as interested in this announcement as are those who are present in the Lord's house," etc.

Many radio broadcasts originate directly from the studio. It is the feeling of the writer that such broadcasts are most effective when there is no one present except those participating in the broadcast, because programs of this type demand an entirely different technique from those where the preacher speaks also to a visible audience. The presence of listeners in the studio will be liable to cause the speaker to vary his technique to avoid ignoring them and thus deprive the radio listener of that feeling which comes when a message is addressed directly and primarily to him.

In the broadcast from the studio the preacher should seem to speak to each individual listener in a direct and personal way as if he were carrying on a person-to-person conversation with him. The radio preacher does not think of the total audience of hundreds or thousands who may be listening to his broadcast. He thinks rather of the individual member of that audience. Some preachers find that it is helpful to have one person sit in front of them as they speak and address their remarks directly to that one individual. To the preacher with imagination this is not necessary. He can talk directly to the microphone as if the microphone were an individual. The radio listeners will be hearing the broadcasts as individuals, seated in small groups or alone near their radios. They should never be "preached" to but rather talked with.

PREPARING THE RADIO MESSAGE

For most studio broadcasts the message will be brief, as the time of the broadcast is usually limited to fifteen or thirty minutes. Of course, there are some broadcasts which are longer. However, a brief message, even on a long broadcast, is preferable to a lengthy sermon. Should the radio program be even an hour in length it will be advisable to have two or three brief messages interspersed with the musical portion of the program rather than to attempt to preach one long sermon. In any case, bear in mind the amount of time allotted for the message, but in an effort to hold to that time be careful that you do not make the message too brief. Inexperienced radio speakers will be surprised to note that as a general thing they will speak more rapidly on the air than they realize. It is well, therefore, to have an extra story or illustration which can be inserted effectively somewhere near the close of the message or to have at hand a poem which can be read there if one finds that his material is used up and that he still has time left to be filled.

The radio sermon should be simple. That does not mean it should be elementary or childish, but rather that it should be couched in simple, ordinary language and not in flowery oratorical phrases. Translate theological terms into the language which the average listener uses and understands. Speak *to* your audience. Do not preach *down to* them.

Controversial matters are out of place in the radio sermon. Present a positive Gospel or Scriptural message, avoiding unimportant denominational twists and sectarian issues.

Most doctrines can be dealt with in such a manner as not to give offense. Since most of the controversy upon such subjects is due to the use of labels and terms which have a peculiar connotation and, therefore, produce unnecessary antagonism, the preacher should exercise care in his choice of terms, so as to avoid hostile reactions. An honest preacher, if he tries in his own mind to be fair and not air his own prejudices and ride his own hobby, can preach upon almost any legitimate subject without arousing antagonism and doing harm to the cause and hurting his influence as a radio speaker.

A radio ministry should always be on the positive side. A preacher who permits himself to be drawn into a controversy with another speaker will hurt his ministry. No man on the air has the right to attack Jews, Catholics, or any other religious group, nor has he a right to attack any individual personally. A radio broadcast affords a wonderful opportunity to exalt the Lord Jesus Christ, to preach the Gospel, and to win souls. It offers a means of instructing men and women in the truth of God's Word. Satan must delight in seeing men turn aside from so high a privilege and waste such an opportunity.

The radio preacher should use concrete material, and include in his broadcast as much illustrative matter as possible, particularly that which has a high degree of human interest and dramatic value. The preacher who is gifted in the dramatization of ideas and in the use of suspense and imagination will find abundant use for such talent in the preparation of radio messages.

A radio message should progress steadily. The listener should have the feeling that the preacher knows where he is going and is on his way there, with a minimum of delays and detours. There are, however, some exceptions to this general rule. Once in a great while a radio preacher appears who seems able simply to sit down and chat with his audience aimlessly and hold their interest and attention. However, such ministers are rare, and for the average preacher to attempt such technique, or rather attempt to speak with such lack of technique and purpose, would be fatal to the success of his broadcast.

More than in almost any other phase of public speaking stereotyped phrases and speech mannerisms show up on the radio. The effective preacher does not use such terms as "out in radio land," "my unseen listeners," etc., and he avoids monotonous repetitions.

TECHNIQUE OF RADIO DELIVERY

Many radio stations insist that a manuscript of every message be submitted in advance to the studio. The preacher is expected to read his message from the manuscript when the program goes on the air. While the reason for such a procedure is, from the standpoint of the station, quite valid, it is doubtful that it does not deprive the program of spontaneity and life. Unquestionably in most cases a broadcast will have greater literary value if the message is read from the manuscript than if it is spoken extemporaneously or from an outline. The question is whether literary value is to be preferred to spontaneity and naturalness in delivery.

Should the preacher be required to read his message, or should he prefer to do so, he must, to be a successful radio preacher, acquire the ability to read the manuscript in such a fashion that he does not seem to his hearers to be reading it. He should be so familiar with the manuscript that he can concentrate upon the content and material of the message rather than upon the words which make it up. Some successful radio speakers have developed their own system of marking a manuscript in order to achieve apparent ease and spontaneity in reading it. A radio preacher might do well to try to work out for himself such a system and see whether or not its use is helpful. In any case, no individual who reads a word at a time will ever successfully present written material on the radio.

There are a number of varieties of microphones, each possessing its own degree of sensitivity. The distance which the speaker maintains from one type will not be right for another. He will do well, therefore, to ask the announcer or engineer to run a test of his voice to determine what distance he should remain from the microphone.

It is important to remain at this proper distance from the microphone throughout the message and to keep the head turned toward the "mike." If a manuscript is used, the speaker should beware of lifting his head so that some of his words are spoken toward the microphone and some down toward the manuscript. Such a procedure will cause sudden and sharp changes in volume. A fairly steady level of vocal power should be maintained, as sudden increases may cause "blasting," and decreases may cause a few words or sentences to be missed altogether.

In radio, vocal variety and interest should depend more upon *progress* and *pitch* than upon *punch* or *pause,* though the latter may be used to some extent. However, pauses should not be so frequent or of so long duration on the radio as in the pulpit. The preacher should seek for a quality of ease and naturalness in radio speaking which will enable the hearers to concentrate upon what he is saying and not upon how he is saying it. He must not be slovenly and indistinct in speech, but in his effort to avoid this, he should be careful not to develop a stilted and artificial form of utterance.

As a general rule, low-pitched voices broadcast more satisfactorily than high voices and in certain cases even a slightly husky quality of voice is an asset to a radio speaker. A radio preacher, while not neglecting the use of the full range of his voice, should particularly rely upon the lower register. He should seek also for vocal warmth and color.

In planning the religious program, one should consider the hour of the broadcast. Some programs are most effective when presented at certain time of day. A program put on the air early in the morning should be quite different from a late night program. The one should be inspirational to give the hearers a feeling of strength and confidence in the Lord with which they can go into the problems and difficulties of the new day. It should be particularly cheerful in character, and while not marked by the professional "pep-you-up-for-the-day" quality of a breakfast-foods broadcast, it should be set in a "major key." A bedtime broadcast, on the other hand, should be quiet and restful, emphasizing the peace which can be found in the Lord, resting in His love. Both programs can exalt Christ, but each presents Him in a different aspect.

Bible-teaching programs are usually more effective after nine o'clock in the morning, and before six in the afternoon. The evangelistic broadcast is also suited for these hours, and possibly even more particularly for the early hours of the evening.

It is customary in almost all types of radio programs to have a theme melody to introduce the program and a signature melody to take the program off the air. There is a good reason for such practice, and it may well be followed in the religious broadcast. Some well-known old hymn tune will lend itself ideally to such a purpose. The melody used for the theme and the signature may be the same, or different melodies may be used. Some thought should be given to the type of broadcast and the time of the broadcast in the selection of good thematic music. "When Morning Gilds the Skies," or "Holy, Holy, Holy," would be suitable for an early morning broadcast, for example; and "Abide with Me," and "Now the Day is Over," for a late evening program. One of the great evangelistic radio programs heard for many years over a number of stations chose as its theme the song "Jesus Saves."

There is great room for improvement in the quality of the music on many of the religious broadcasts heard throughout America. The sort of music presented on many of these broadcasts is a reflection upon the Lord's work. A screechy soprano who sings off key, and so-called quartets made up sometimes of one woman and three men, accompanied, more or less, by the searching fingers of a groping pianist, butcher the old hymns and Gospel songs. Better no music at all than such barbarisms.

Every religious broadcast that includes music should have good vocalists, even if it is necessary to pay them, and if only one can be afforded, better one good paid singer than four or five poor ones whom nobody *would* pay!

The music of a broadcast should be selected with the theme of the message in mind and there will then be some central thread upon which the entire broadcast can be strung together, and the music should be well rehearsed and timed in advance of the broadcast. There is no excuse for a last-minute rushing into a studio and picking out songs at random and giving them a quick run-through before time to go on the air. No secular broadcast, whether for the purpose of advertising pills or beer, is so carelessly thrown together.

In a well-prepared program there will be definite points of climax; there will be elements of novelty. Variety should be sought for in the way in which hymns are announced and introduced and in the manner in which the various parts of the broadcast are connected. This will require more than casual attention.

STUDIO ETIQUETTE

In conclusion, it might be well to suggest that there are at least three matters of studio etiquette which the participants in a religious broadcast should bear in mind. The first of these is that the studio should be vacated as soon as the broadcast goes off the air. Another group may be waiting to come in to rehearse. A second point of studio custom to be regarded is that microphones and studio equipment should not be moved without the permission of the announcer or the engineer. They are usually glad to be of any assistance possible when a change is desired. Finally, stay out of the control room unless invited in or when auditioning speakers or singers for your own program or when rehearsing a broadcast for the production for which you are responsible.

BIBLIOGRAPHY

Abbott, Waldo, *Handbook of Broadcasting*. New York: Mc-Graw-Hill, 1937. 424 pp.

Anderson, Virgil Antris, *Training the Speaking Voice*. New York: Oxford, 1942. 387 pp.

Blackwood, Andrew W., *Preaching from the Bible*. New York: Abingdon-Cokesbury Press, 1941. 247 pp.

Bodine, William Budd, *Some Hymns and Hymn Writers*. Philadelphia: The John C. Winston Company, 1907. 458 pp.

Borden, Richard C., and Alvin C. Busse, *Speech Correction*. New York: F. S. Crofts & Company, 1937. 295 pp.

Broadus, John, *A Treatise on the Preparation and Delivery of Sermons*. New York: Harper & Brothers Publishers, 1926. 562 pp.

Brooks, Phillips, *Lectures on Preaching*. New York: E. P. Dutton and Company, 1894. 281 pp.

Brown, Theron, and Hezekiah Butterworth, *The Story of the Hymns and Tunes*. New York: George H. Doran, 1906. 564 pp.

Burrage, Henry, *Baptist Hymn Writers and Their Hymns*. Portland, Maine: Brown Thurston and Company, 1888. 682 pp.

Cantril, Hadley, and Gordon W. Allport, *The Psychology of Radio*. New York: Peter Smith, 1941. 276 pp.

Carlile, John S., *Production and Direction of Radio Programs*. New York: Prentice-Hall, Inc., 1940. 397 pp.

Cuyler, Theodore L., *The Young Preacher*. New York: Fleming H. Revell Company, 1893. 111 pp.

Dargan, Edwin Charles, *The Art of Preaching in the Light of its History*. Nashville: South Baptist Sunday School Board, 1922. 247 pp.

Doddridge, Philip, *The Rise and Progress of Religion in the Soul*. London: Ward, Lock, and Co., 1878. 192 pp.

Duffield, Samuel Willoughby, *English Hymns*. New York: Funk & Wagnalls Co., 1886. 675 pp.

Dunlap, Orrin E., *Talking on the Radio*. New York: Greenberg, 1936. 216 pp.

Forsyth, P. T., *Positive Preaching and Modern Mind*. New York: A. C. Armstrong & Son, 1908. 374 pp.

Foxell, W. J., *Sermon and Preacher*. New York: E. P. Dutton & Co., 1904. 164 pp.

Fuller, David Otis, *C. H. Spurgeon's Sermon Notes*. Grand Rapids: Zondervan Publishing House, 1941. 334 pp.

Gardner, Charles S., *Psychology and Preaching*. New York: The MacMillan Company, 1919. 387 pp.

Garvie, Alfred E., *A Guide to Preachers*. London: Hodder and Stoughton, 1906. 351 pp.

Hallock, G. B. F., *One Hundred Best Sermons for Special Days and Occasions*. New York: Harper & Brothers Publishers, 1923. 562 pp.

Judson, Lyman Spicer, and Andrew Thomas Weaver, *Voice Science*. New York: F. S. Crofts & Company, 1942. 377 pp.

Julian, John, *A Dictionary of Hymnology*. London: John Murray, 1925. 1768 pp.

Kidder, Daniel P., *A Treatise on Homiletics*. New York: Carlon and Lanahan, 1868. 503 pp.

Kleiser, Grenville, compiler, *The World's Great Sermons*. New York: Funk & Wagnalls Company, 1908. 10 Vols.

Lazarfeld, Paul F., *Radio and the Printed Page*. New York: Duell, Sloan, and Pearce, 1940. 354 pp.

McCutchan, Robert Gary, *Our Hymnody*. New York: The Methodist Book Concern, 1937. 619 pp.

McGill, Earle, *Radio Directing*. New York: McGraw-Hill Book Company, Inc., 1940. 370 pp.

Monroe, Alan H., *Principles and Types of Speech*. New York: Scott, Foresman and Company, 1939. 546 pp.

Montgomery, R. Ames, *Preparing Preachers to Preach*. Grand Rapids: Zondervan Publishing House, 1939. 249 pp.

Morgan, G. Campbell, *Preaching*. New York: Fleming H. Revell Company, 1937. 90 pp.

Mosher, Joseph A., *The Production of Correct Speech Sounds*. Boston: Expression Company, 1929. 198 pp.

Ninde, Edward S., *The Story of the American Hymn*. New York: The Abingdon Press, 1921. 429 pp.

Noyes, Morgan Phelps, *Preaching the Word of God*. New York: Charles Scribner's Sons, 1943. 219 pp.

Nutter, Charles S., and Wilbur F. Tillett, *The Hymns and Hymn Writers*. New York: The Methodist Book Concern, 1911. 499 pp.

Parrish, Wayland Maxfield, *Reading Aloud*. New York: T. Nelson & Sons, 1932. 401 pp.

Phelps, Austin, *Men and Books*. New York: Charles Scribner's Sons, 1892. 354 pp.

———, *The Theory of Preaching*. New York: Charles Scribner's Sons, 1892. 601 pp.

Pierson, Arthur T., *The Divine Art of Preaching*. New York: The Baker and Taylor Company, 1892. 156 pp.

Ray, Jeff D., *Expository Preaching*. Grand Rapids: Zondervan Publishing House, 1940. 123 pp.

Robinson, Charles Seymour, *Annotations upon Popular Hymns*. New York: Hunt and Eaton, 1893. 581 pp.

Russell, G. Oscar, *Speech and Voice*. New York: The MacMillan Company, 1931. 250 pp.

Sarett, Lew, and William Trufort Foster, *Basic Principles of Speech*. Boston: Houghton Mifflin Company, 1936. 577 pp.

Shedd, William G. T., *Homiletics and Pastoral Theology*. New York: Charles Scribner's Sons, 1867. 429 pp.

Simpson, Matthew, *Lectures on Preaching*. New York: Phillips & Hunt, 1879. 336 pp.

Smith, Arthur H., *Preachers and Preaching*. Philadelphia: The United Lutheran Publication House, 1925. 145 pp.

Smith, H. Augustine, *Lyric Religion*. New York: The Century Company, 1931. 517 pp.

Spurgeon, C. H., *The Art of Illustration*. New York: Wilbur B. Ketcham, 1894. 205 pp.

Stanley, Douglas, *The Science of Voice*. New York: Carl Fischer, Inc., 1939. 384 pp.

Stevens, Abel, *Essays on the Preaching Required by the Times*. New York: Carlton & Phillips, 1856. 266 pp.

Tigert, John J., *The Preacher Himself*. Nashville, Tennessee: House of the M. E. Church, South, 1899. 200 pp.

Watters, Philip M., *Peter Cartwright*. New York: Eaton & Mains, 1910. 128 pp.

West, Robert, and others, *The Rehabilitation of Speech*. New York: Harper & Brothers, 1937. 475 pp.

Woolbert, Charles Henry, and Severina E. Nelson, *The Art of Interpretative Speech*. New York: F. S. Crofts & Company, 1934. 541 pp.

Young, William Henry, *How to Preach with Power*. Athens, Georgia: The How Publishing Company, 1897. 365 pp.